BETWEEN THE LINES

Page 2 of *Byzantium*

JON STALLWORTHY

BETWEEN THE LINES

YEATS'S POETRY

IN THE MAKING

OXFORD

AT THE CLARENDON PRESS

1963

303078

Oxford University Press, Amen House, London, E.C.4

GLASGOW   NEW YORK   TORONTO   MELBOURNE   WELLINGTON
BOMBAY   CALCUTTA   MADRAS   KARACHI   LAHORE   DACCA
CAPE TOWN   SALISBURY   NAIROBI   IBADAN   ACCRA
KUALA LUMPUR   HONG KONG

© *Oxford University Press 1963*

PRINTED IN GREAT BRITAIN

Accursed who brings to light of day
The writings I have cast away!
But blessed he that stirs them not
And lets the kind worm take the lot!

W. B. YEATS

Lord, have mercy upon us.

ACKNOWLEDGEMENTS are due to Mrs. W. B. Yeats for permission to reproduce copyright manuscripts in her possession, and to Mrs. W. B. Yeats and Messrs. Macmillan & Company, publishers of W. B. Yeats's *Collected Poems*, for permission to reproduce copyright poems.

PREFACE

I AM afraid that Yeats would have deplored my choice of subject. He would probably have regarded me as the magician at a children's party regards the inevitable small boy who explains to his friends that 'of course the top hat has a false bottom'. I must therefore, in all humility, offer the case for my defence.

Despite his taste for sumptuous manuscript books, there can be little doubt that Yeats did not generally intend his manuscripts to be published and anatomized. Many rough drafts he actually tore up, and these have only survived through the vigilance of Mrs. Yeats, who rescued them from the waste-paper basket. There may be some who question the ethics of this, and indeed of anatomizing also. If, however, the motive is a reverent curiosity, and the result an enlarged understanding of the man and his work, I submit that the end justifies a slight irregularity in the means. Certainly my own understanding of the poems and my admiration for the craftsman-ship of the poet, have increased immeasurably from contact with his manuscripts: and I have done my best to handle them reverently. Had Harvey not practised dissection he would never have dis-covered the circulation of the blood. With this thought for consola-tion, I have chosen to disregard the curse, and 'bring to light of day' the hidden workings of certain poems.

By 'handling the manuscripts reverently' I mean that I have tried to keep a sense of proportion between Yeats's text and my commentary. Although I have profited, to a larger or lesser extent, from a great many of the books and articles listed in G. B. Saul's *Prolegomena to the Study of Yeats's Poems*, I have avoided, wherever possible, discussion of earlier critical writings. These, with their theories and counter-theories, could so easily obscure the patterns of the material itself, that I felt it would be wiser to exclude them. Like a restorer of stained-glass windows, I have tried to fix a multi-tude of fragments in place with a minimum of lead.

My choice of poems has been largely determined by the manuscript material available: for many interesting poems, like 'Easter 1916' for example, have uninteresting manuscripts. I did have one hare in view, however, as I hunted through them, and this, to some extent, has influenced my selection. The nature of that hare will appear in the following chapters.

I have no doubt that in a very few years the manuscripts, through which I tiptoed so happily with my magnifying glass, will have had all their rough places made smooth by disciplined squads of research workers, acting on radioed instructions from their professors, assistant professors, and professorial assistants. Science, I am afraid, will lay bare many sins of omission and commission in my transcriptions, and in their ordering. Photographers will prepare sumptuous facsimiles in many volumes, white-coated chemists will analyse the inks, and computers will reveal blinding statistical truths concerning Yeats's use of the full-stop/period. There will be battles fought over every difficult reading, more intense I suspect than any experienced by the poet who wrote it. And when there is no more to read between the lines, when every valley has been exalted, and when every research worker has the doctorate that is his due, it will all be very stimulating and satisfactory, provided that the finished poems have kept their colours in the wash. It is a risk, but a risk undertaken every time a critic puts pen to paper; and I think Yeats's poems will keep their colours. I hope then to be forgiven for rushing in ahead of the angels, with only a magnifying glass, and no rubber gloves.

I should like to express my gratitude to Sir Maurice Bowra, whose enthusiasm filled my sail; to Miss Helen Gardner and Mr. John Bryson, who between them corrected a great many navigational errors; and, above all, to Mrs. W. B. Yeats, whose generosity provided me with a cargo which alone justifies the voyage. I want also to thank my wife, who in her capacity as crew, mate, and pilot, did more than anyone to keep the ship afloat; and to her I dedicate this book.

J. S.

Oxford 1961

CONTENTS

INTRODUCTION

YEATS began his 'sedentary trade' when still a boy. At school he never won a prize for an essay because of his bad spelling, and at home it would seem that his poetry came in for certain well-directed criticisms. His father, writing of 'this youth of eighteen' in a letter to Edward Dowden, said: 'his bad metres arise very much from his composing in a loud voice, manipulating of course the quantities to his own taste'.[1] In 1885, at the age of twenty, he first achieved the dignity of print. The untitled stanzas beginning 'A man has the fields of heaven,' appeared in the March number of the *Dublin University Review*, a magazine which was to contain several of his early poems.

As late as 1926 Yeats could speak of his 'intense unnatural labour that reduces composition to four or five lines a day'.[2] He was neither born with, achieved, nor had thrust upon him, that facility which characterizes the work of many other poets, notably in the Romantic era. To Katherine Tynan he wrote: 'I envy your power of writing stray snatches of verse. I cannot do it at all. With me everything is premeditated for a long time. When I am away in the country and easy in my mind I have much inspiration of the moment—never here'[3] (London). Again he wrote to her of 'The Wanderings of Oisin': 'It beset me day and night. Not that I ever wrote more than a few lines in a day. But those few lines took me hours. All the rest of the time I walked about the roads thinking of it.'[4] He elaborates this in his essay on 'Speaking to the Psaltery': 'Like every other poet, I spoke verses in a kind of chant when I was making them, and sometimes, when I was alone on a country road, I would speak them in a loud chanting voice.' No doubt he was thinking in particular of Wordsworth. Shepherds and dalesmen, reputedly, were often surprised and even alarmed by the gaunt,

---

[1] C. Bax, ed., *Florence Farr, Bernard Shaw and W. B. Yeats*, Cuala Press, 1941, p. 42.
[2] A. Wade, ed., *The Letters of W. B. Yeats*, 1954, p. 710.
[3] Ibid., p. 107.
[4] Ibid., p. 87.

B

muttering figure that would overtake them out of the lakeland mist.

The last entry in Manuscript Book A (with the exception of two drafted 'lists of contents') is evidently the preliminary prose draft of a poem.[1] It is entitled simply 'Subject for a lyric'.

O my beloved you only are

not moved by my songs

Which you only understand

You only know that it it is

of you I sing when I tell

of the swan on the water

of the eagle in the heavens

of the faun in the wood.

Others weep but your eyes

are dry.

II

O my beloved. How happy

I was that day when you

came here from the

railway, & set your hair

a right in my looking glass

& then sat with me at

my table, & ~~the~~ lay resting

in my big chair. I am

---

[1] See pp. 11 and 12 for my methods of transcription. Ellmann quotes the first two stanzas in *Yeats/The Man and the Masks*, 1949, p. 161.

like the children, O my

beloved & I play at

~~*Life &*~~ *marriage. I play*
                with
~~*at*~~ *images of the life*

you will not give to me O

my ~~*cruel one*~~ *cruel one.*

III

I put away all the romances.

How care I now of queens

& of noble women, whose

very dust is full of sorrow,

are they not all but my

beloved whispering to me.

I wait at the woods. I

hear the cry of the birds

& the cry of the deer

& I hear the wind among the

reeds, but I put my hands

over my ears for were not

they my beloved whispering to

me. O my beloved why do

you whisper to me of sorrow

always.

IIII

O my beloved what were verse to me

If you were not then to listen

& yet all my verses are little to you.

Your eyes set upon upon far magnificence

Upon impossible heroism

Have made you blind and have made you deaf

You gave your country a flame

I(   ) you have no thing but

these verses, that are but like

mire & leaves in the middle of a crowd.

Other eyes fill with tears but

yours are dry.

As early as 1895, and it may be earlier, Yeats seems to have followed a pattern of composition which was to vary little for the rest of his life: prose draft, rough verse drafts, fair copy, magazine publication, and then further revisions for the first printing in book form. Even that was often not the last word. Mr. Mark, of Macmillan's publishing company, who nursed many of the poet's books through the press, has been presented by Mrs. Yeats with her husband's own copy of the first edition of *The Wanderings of Oisin and Other Poems*. This contains numerous pencilled corrections of the printed text which were incorporated in subsequent editions. It is interesting to note that this book was originally stolen from Woburn Buildings, and rediscovered by Mrs. Yeats in a bookshop in the Charing Cross Road, from which she bought it for 2s. 6d.

Two qualities in particular dominate Yeats's habits of composition. The first is perseverance. 'I, since I was seventeen,' he

wrote to Lady Gregory, 'have never begun a story or poem or essay of any kind that I have not finished.'[1] Nor was he easily satisfied, as is shown by the many, struggling, scored-out drafts of his essays, plays, and, most of all, his poetry. 'The correction of prose, because it has no fixed laws, is endless, a poem comes right with a click like a closing box', he wrote to Dorothy Wellesley:[2] but true though this may be in general terms, it throws a somewhat distorting light upon his own work. Such of the prose manuscripts as I have had access to, reveal considerably less draft working than many poems of shorter length. To describe the poet at work, a closer analogy than the 'click of a closing box' would perhaps be that of a locksmith opening a safe. He is searching for the right combination, and as the dials turn slowly beneath his fingers, the trained ear listens for the click of cogs slipping into place. One by one the numbers come up, until finally the door swings open upon a completed poem.

Important as the patience and perseverance that keep his fingers turning the dials, is the critical ear that can distinguish between a right and a wrong sound. As he explained to Fiona Macleod: 'I do so much of my work by the critical, rather than the imaginative faculty'.[3] Elsewhere he wrote of 'my kind of critical mind'.[4] This, surprisingly enough, is little evidenced in his assessment of *other* people's work. The 1936 *Oxford Book of Modern Verse* is a classic example of one man's monumental prejudice. Both the selection and the introduction—although a triumph of incisive and sustained rhetoric—should be read for the light they cast on Yeats, rather than for an informed guide to the subject. Human sympathies were inclined to warp his literary judgement, and the *Oxford Book of Modern Verse* is today more of interest as a gallery of Yeats's friends, than one of modern poets.

> Think where man's glory most begins and ends
> And say my glory was I had such friends.

The poets of The Cheshire Cheese have their place in literary history, but neither Dowson nor Johnson merit that which their editor allotted them. The Irish Brigade is there in review order;

[1] Wade, *Letters*, p. 345. [2] D. Wellesley, ed., *Letters on Poetry*, 1940, p. 24.
[3] Wade, *Letters*, p. 358. [4] Ibid., p. 827.

Oliver St. John Gogarty, for example, with seventeen poems. Wilfred Owen, on the other hand, does not appear at all because, declared the pontiff, 'passive suffering is not a theme for poetry'. Again, a weakness for poetesses, of more distinguished personality than talent, moves him to include Lady Gregory, Lady Dorothy Wellesley, and Margot Ruddock:

> That crazed girl improvising her music,
> Her poetry, dancing upon the shore.

This, however, is ground well trodden, but none the less important for the contrast it makes with the critical acumen Yeats brought to bear on his own work. He is capable of a detachment rare, if not unique, in a self-confessed romantic poet, who wrote so constantly out of his own experience. Where words are concerned he has almost perfect pitch. If word, verse, or stanza makes a wrong sound, unhesitatingly he crosses it out; and seldom does his ear betray him into a change for the worse. Personally I regret the dropping of the first line of his epitaph. One morning when, as was his habit, he was working in bed, Mrs. Yeats heard him call, and entered his room to see him hurl to the floor in disgust a book of essays on Rilke. He did not then, as some people have reported, write in the margin of the book, but on a scrap of paper, and afterwards in a letter to Dorothy Wellesley, the lines:

> Draw rein; draw breath.
> Cast a cold eye
> On life, on death.
> Horseman pass by.[1]

I would also have supported Mrs. Yeats in her valiant efforts to have reinstated the original version of:

> I think it better that in times like these
> A poet's mouth be silent, . . .

which was:

> I think it better that in times like these
> We poets keep our mouths shut, . . .[2]

The savage colloquialism is more in harmony with the poet's true attitude towards his subject.

[1] Wade, *Letters*, p. 913.   [2] 'On being asked for a War Poem'.

Time and again, however, in the manuscripts he may be found groping, perhaps over a whole page, to put five or six words into their one and only correct order. So painstaking is this process that it is not difficult to see how sometimes he was unable to write 'more than a few lines in a day'. Not that he was always as slow as this. We have Mrs. Yeats's story of him in 1921 hurrying from a waiting train to get paper from the Euston Hotel, and reappearing a moment or two later with 'The Wheel':[1]

> Through winter-time we call on spring,
> And through the spring on summer call,
> And when the abounding hedges sing
> Declare that winter's best of all;
> And after that there's nothing good
> Because the spring-time has not come—
> Nor know that what disturbs our blood
> Is but its longing for the tomb.

Railways, for some reason, seem to have stimulated him. Writing to Lady Gregory about the poem 'Old Memory', he said:

I made it when shut up in a railway train coming from Canada. I think a railroad train a good place to write when the journey is long enough. One will exhaust the scenery in the first two or three hours and the newspaper in the second two or three hours (even an American newspaper), and towards the end of the day one can hardly help oneself, but one has begun to write. Indeed I think that if some benevolent government would only shut one up in the smoking car of a railway train and send one across the world one would really write two or three dozen lyrics in the year.[2]

Far from having perfect pitch where music was concerned, Yeats was notoriously tone-deaf. To Monk Gibbon he wrote:

I have no ear—don't know one tune from another. I cannot make head or tail of anything but little folk songs to which (I) listen as if they were something said. Music impresses me but I can no more judge of its quality than I can of the qualities of thunder or the sound of wind.[3]

In a letter written in 1902 to the Editor of the *Saturday Review* he went further, saying: 'I am afraid I even dislike music.'[4] How

---

[1] J. Hall and M. Steinmann, eds., *The Permanence of Yeats*, 1950, p. 301.
[2] Wade, *Letters*, p. 427.   [3] M. Gibbon, *The Masterpiece and the Man*, 1959, p. 133.
[4] Wade, *Letters*, p. 366.

then are we to reconcile this with F. R. Higgins's recollection of Yeats:

telling me some years back that most of his poems were composed to some vague tune, some lilt. Indeed, when we were together, he sang in his own uncertain, shy way, some of these poems. Whenever these poems were again repeated, at later dates, he always sang them to the same halting lilt.[1]

All poetry, Yeats frequently said, was song. Mrs. Yeats told the late G. D. P. Allt that her husband, 'sang his proofs and often forgot to consider whether song and printed word corresponded'.[2] I think the answer lies in the difference between rhythm and pitch, or—in terms of a graph—the spacing of sounds on a horizontal plane, as against the intervals on a vertical plane. As if in compensation for his insensitivity to pitch, Yeats from his first beginnings as a poet had more of the great gift of rhythm than any of his contemporaries. The importance that he himself set by rhythm was considerable, as he shows in the essay 'The Symbolism of Poetry', written in 1900:

The purpose of rhythm, it has always seemed to me, is to prolong the moment of contemplation, the moment when we are both asleep and awake, which is the one moment of creation, by hushing us with an alluring monotony, while it holds us waking by variety, to keep us in that state of perhaps real trance, in which the mind liberated from the pressure of the will is unfolded in symbols.

The rhythm of many of the earlier poems is too hypnotic. In these, as in much of his prose, Yeats's orchestra is unbalanced. The percussion and wind sections give the strings no chance. The listener is aware of grandeur and beauty, but because his intellect is lulled to sleep, he receives no lasting impression of definite meaning. This, of course, was a deliberate policy among the poets of the 90's, and Yeats was one of the very few to break free from the Pre-Raphaelite spell. His association first of all with the theatre, and then with Ezra Pound, taught him to reshape his style on more colloquial principles. Dowsonesque rhythms, like those of 'He bids his Beloved be at Peace' or part III of 'The Wanderings

[1] S. L. Gwynn, ed., *Scattering Branches*, 1940, p. 150.
[2] P. Allt, 'Yeats and the Revision of His Early Verse', *Hermathena*, nos. 63–66, p. 101.

of Oisin', he wisely abandoned. A passionate poet cannot be trammelled with too formal a verse pattern. If the new wine is good it will break the old bottle. In 1903 he wrote to Lady Gregory: 'My work has got far more masculine. It has more salt in it.'[1] Between *The Wind among the Reeds* and *In the Seven Woods* the changing style is already visible. He was beginning to use the shorter octosyllabic line more than the standard pentametre, and with a marked increase in compression. Rhythm becomes servant rather than master of meaning: stress falls more often on the significant words, and no longer with the regularity of the metronome. Diction, like metre, grows more colloquial, and in revision all literary archaisms are pruned away. For example, 'starn' in line 33 of 'Adam's Curse' is emended to 'stars', and in line 2 of 'The Ragged Wood', 'leman' is altered to 'lady'.

The manuscripts of many of the poems in *Michael Robartes and the Dancer* (1921) have been torn in two. Happily for the literary Resurrection Men, when the poet committed them to his waste-paper basket, Mrs. Yeats was at hand to recover and piece them together again. I suspect, however, that the drafts of many poems written before his marriage in 1917 had no such reprieve from the waste-paper basket. Of those written subsequently, there remains —thanks to Mrs. Yeats—a mass of manuscript and typescript material. 'Maze' would perhaps be a better word than 'mass', and anyone entering without his ball of twine will be lost in a moment.

The first difficulty is Yeats's handwriting, which over the years grew worse with his increasing myopia. Although quite capable of writing legibly, as his fair copies show—even as late as 'The Black Tower'—the preliminary workings of a poem were generally written for no eye but his own. Latterly, Mrs. Yeats told me, he frequently could not himself read what he had written: there is much that she has never been able to read, even with a strong magnifying glass. As he grew older he wrote, I believe, often with no intention of reading what was before him on the page: his fingers were simply turning the dials. He did not watch them, but rather listened to the stirring of the cog-wheels in his brain. He

[1] Wade, *Letters*, p. 397.

was in fact *thinking* on paper, and this gives his manuscripts their especial fascination. Reading them, one seems to be at his elbow, with the great voice chanting in one's ears. For the present, one example must suffice. It is to be found on p. 39 of Manuscript Book D. I take this to be the first appearance of 'Ribh considers Christian Love insufficient':

~~Hatred I seek~~

~~Love is of god & comes unsaught~~

I c(   )
                which
I cannot study love is of god

~~I study hatred with great diligence~~

~~I cannot stu~~

~~I do not seek for love love comes~~ unsaught

I do not seek for love nor study it

It comes unsaught & passes human wit

~~Because it comes from~~ god

I seek I study all great diligence
        That's a passion that I know in my control
~~Hatred for that is in my own control~~

~~The only thing that is in my control~~
   ~~My hatred that~~ (   ) that are purges of the soul
~~Hatred ; that may~~ purges of the soul
   ~~May—I~~ (   ) it nothing
~~Must leave it nothing~~ but bare mind & sense

~~That leaves me~~ I (   ) nothing there but mind & sense

Why do I hate man woman or event ;

Hatred delivered from the false light lent

By terror shows what things are (   )
     ~~What nature to the soul~~ (   )

> ~~What nature to the soul,~~ *age shows at last*
>
> ~~What things are nature to the soul at last~~
>   *that*
> *How* ~~the~~ *shall walk when all such things are past*
>   ~~How that has~~
> ~~Or how it~~ *walked before such things began*
>
>   *Or how it*

Here he reached the foot of the page and, turning the book on its side, wrote along the right-hand edge of the page:

> *Hatred that* (   ) *a besom in the soul*
>
> *And leaves it nothing but bare mind & sense*

The handwriting, particularly in preliminary drafts of the *Last Poems*, travels the no man's land between longhand and shorthand. To touch upon just a few of its eccentricities: a symbol like ⊃ can be a capital *I*, or *O*, or occasionally an ampersand. Small *t*'s are frequently uncrossed and *i*'s undotted; *t* can mean 'to'; 'not' and 'but' are sometimes indistinguishable, as are also: 'then', 'there', 'their', 'the', 'this', 'these', 'those'; likewise: 'in', 'on', 'or', 'an'. The suffix *-ed* is often no more than an upward curve ⌐; *-ing* no more than a downward curve ⌐. A final *s* is frequently omitted or unrecognizable, so that the singular form of a noun cannot be distinguished from the plural.

By now it should be clear that anyone transcribing *exactly* what he saw on the page before him would ultimately be faced with gibberish. A transcriber must accordingly at times exercise the licence of a translator for his findings to be intelligible to any that have not spent long hours studying the manuscripts. If, as in drafts of 'The Black Tower', Yeats has frequently written 'mount' where in my opinion he means 'mountain' (which alone will scan, and is supported by the final text), I have transcribed it as 'mountain'. I have deliberately avoided the convention by which one would write 'mount(ain)', as being more a distraction than a help. Brackets I have used only to denote something that I cannot read; if that something happens also to be crossed out, it will appear in my transcription as ~~(————)~~. There can be no confusion with brackets in the poet's own punctuation, because he 'disliked a dash and detested brackets'.[1]

Where Yeats was uncertain about a line of verse he sometimes put a broken line underneath it. This can also indicate italics, though it seldom does, and the transcriber must decide which is intended by the context: I only record the broken line that denotes uncertainty or dissatisfaction. The poet had four chief ways of crossing out. Most common was the simple straight line through a word or words. He also used the 'barbed wire' or wavy line, and occasionally—if particularly dissatisfied with something—he blocked it out savagely in ink. In my transcriptions these three methods of crossing out are all represented by a single straight line through the offending words, as: ~~Hatred I seek~~. A fourth mark of the poet's disfavour was the line, or lines, drawn vertically or diagonally through a passage. These I do not attempt to reproduce, but simply state that certain verses are so crossed out. While putting verse quotations from a printed source in single spaced roman, all my transcriptions from manuscript are in double spaced italic. This both distinguishes between them, and enables the corrections to be shown which Yeats, almost without exception, wrote *over* the line corrected. Thus, where in my transcription two lines are divided by a single space only, the upper and inset line is a correction of the lower.

I have tried throughout to preserve the character and flavour of the manuscripts, while at the same time reducing them to some semblance of order. The occasional quaint spelling I have retained —see 'unsaught' above—and have put in no more punctuation than to restore the lapsed apostrophe in 'he's' or 'it's'. Yeats told Robert Bridges in 1915: 'I do not understand stops. I write my work so completely for the ear that I feel helpless when I have to measure pauses by stops and commas.'[2] Again, as late as 1932 he wrote to his publisher: 'I have never been able to punctuate properly. I do not think I have ever differed from a correction of yours in punctuation. I suggest that in the remaining volumes you do not query your corrections.'[3] Mrs. Yeats tells a charming story

[1] P. Allt, 'Yeats and the Revision of His Early Verse', *Hermathena*, nos. 63–66, p. 97.
[2] Wade, *Letters*, p. 598.   [3] Unpublished letter to Mr. T. Mark.

of a time when she was taking down a prose passage at her husband's dictation, and after three-quarters of an hour he suddenly said, 'Comma'. Punctuation, in fact, was frequently put in after the words were written, and put in as often by Mrs. Yeats, or the publisher, as by the poet himself. For this reason we should not take the changes in punctuation, listed so scrupulously in the *Variorum*, as necessarily made by Yeats.

Even when a transcriber has to some extent mastered the handwriting, the great problem of the manuscript labyrinth still remains: namely, finding one's way about. The notebooks in particular are a jumbled jig-saw of prose and verse pieces, memoranda, diagrams, and even an occasional horoscope. Nor has the order in which the pieces occur any relevance to their order of composition. For example, in Manuscript Book C there is to be found on page 141 a fair copy of 'The Delphic Oracle upon Plotinus'; while much earlier working-drafts come on pages 236 and 239. Sometimes, for no apparent reason, Yeats would turn his notebook upside down and begin at the other end. Other poems have to be tracked from notebook to rough paper, and back again. Often the Page can follow without difficulty in his Master's steps: on the other hand, there are times when he has no alternative but to trust to his intuition. This is especially the case with poems written in loose-leaf notebooks from which the leaves have subsequently been removed and their sequence lost. Even here there is sometimes a clue, arising from Yeats's habit of writing first on the right-hand page, then adding corrections on the left-hand page, and linking the two with long arrows.

I must make quite clear that the order in which I have pieced the fragments together is my order, and not necessarily the correct one. I have worked on the assumption that where there is a prose draft it should come first, and that the stanzas were built up in the order in which they appear in the first full draft. I am aware that, like many poets, Yeats may have written the last stanza first: sometimes I know he did: but where there is doubt, I have assumed that he wrote them in their eventual order. Other problems in the labyrinth—such as the evidence of different coloured inks—I have attempted to plot as they occur.

Poets are notoriously inconsistent in their habits. Few of them
have worked to such a regular daily pattern as sustained by certain
novelists. In a long lifetime Yeats no doubt varied both his methods
and his routine. He told his sister Lily in 1894:

I am half through the revision of *The Wanderings of Oisin*, now *The
Wanderings of Usheen*. I do the new poems always before dinner and
work at the old one(s) after, and am getting on very slowly.[1]

Eleven years later he wrote from Coole Park:

I have got into my routine here—always my place of industry. After
breakfast Chaucer—garden for twenty minutes—then work from eleven
till two, then lunch, then I fish from three till five, then I read and then
work again at lighter tasks till dinner—after dinner walk. To this I have
added Sandow exercises twice daily.[2]

In the years following his marriage, when most of the poems with
which I am to be concerned were written, much of their early
workings would seem to have taken place simultaneously on paper
and in his head. Then would come a shout for the typewriter,
and Yeats would stand at the typist's elbow, reciting and watching
his poem grow on the roller before him. There might be half a
dozen or more versions (some with carbon copies) typed, corrected,
and generally destroyed, before he was satisfied.

Mrs. Yeats introduced her husband to detective stories. Often
when he was exhausted by his struggle with a stubborn poem, he
would read one of these for half an hour before returning to the
struggle with renewed vigour. I end this introductory section
with a last, amusing illustration of Yeats's gradual adjustment to a
changing world. His wife had for a long time possessed a private
wireless, which he held in scorn as one of the inventions of a
decadent and materialist civilization. Then came the recording of
his first broadcast, and shortly afterwards a package arrived at the
front door. He had ordered himself a fine set, eagerly supervised
its installation, and then sat down to listen. There Mrs. Yeats
found him, leaning forward in his chair with an impatient 'I beg
your pardon?' addressed to an indistinct announcer.

[1] Wade, *Letters*, p. 244.
[2] Ibid., p. 454.

Consideration of the patterns of composition, I reserve till after some examination of the poems themselves.

NOTE

For easy reference I give, at the beginning of each chapter, the *Variorum* texts of the poems there discussed.

I

THE SECOND COMING

•••

1. Turning and turning in the widening gyre
2. The falcon cannot hear the falconer;
3. Things fall apart; the centre cannot hold;
4. Mere anarchy is loosed upon the world,
5. The blood-dimmed tide is loosed, and everywhere
6. The ceremony of innocence is drowned;
7. The best lack all conviction, while the worst
8. Are full of passionate intensity.

9. Surely some revelation is at hand;
10. Surely the Second Coming is at hand.
11. The Second Coming! Hardly are those words out
12. When a vast image out of *Spiritus Mundi*
13. Troubles my sight: somewhere in sands of the desert
14. A shape with lion body and the head of a man,
15. A gaze blank and pitiless as the sun,
16. Is moving its slow thighs, while all about it
17. Reel shadows of the indignant desert birds.
18. The darkness drops again; but now I know
19. That twenty centuries of stony sleep
20. Were vexed to nightmare by a rocking cradle,
21. And what rough beast, its hour come round at last,
22. Slouches towards Bethlehem to be born?

ELLMANN dates this poem January 1919,[1] although it was not published until November 1920, in *The Dial*. Manuscripts in Mrs. Yeats's possession show how large a part the world situation of 1918–19 played in its conception and growth. There are six small, loose-leaf sheets of preliminary manuscript working, and two fair copies, the earlier of which Yeats tore in half and committed to his waste-paper basket: from this Mrs. Yeats recovered it.

'The Second Coming' begins with a tantalizingly illegible prose draft. Of its twelve lines I can read in the first five:

> F. 1r: *Ever more wide sweeping gyre*
>
> *Ever further hawk flies outwards*
>
> · *from the falconer's hand. surely*
>
> (   ) *fallen who*
>
> *when the mob* (   )

In the remaining six lines one word only stands out, in splendid isolation at the opening of line nine: 'Burke'. Below this passage the iambic pentametres begin:

> *intellectual gyre is* (   )
> The ~~gyres grow wider and more~~ *wide*
> *falcon cannot hear*
> The ~~hawk can no more hear~~ *the falconer*
>
> ~~The germans to Russia to the place~~
>
> *The germans are* (   ) *now to Russia come*
>
> *Though every day some innocent has died*
>
> (   ) *& murder*
>
> ⟨————⟩

[1] *The Identity of Yeats*, 1954, p. 290.

C

'Wide' and 'died' on this folio, 'day'/'pay', 'falconer'/'murderer' on F. *2r*, and 'clock'/'dock' on F. *1v* show that the poem was originally to have been in rhyme.

An important alteration is that from 'hawk' to 'falcon'. Ellmann is right when he says:

> The image of the falcon who is out of the falconer's control should not be localized, as some have suggested, as an image of man loose from Christ; Yeats would not have cluttered the poem by referring to Christ both as falconer and as rocking cradle further on.[1]

The falcon has long been a problem. Once, however, we realize that the bird was originally a hawk, we are on familiar territory. As a boy Yeats had often 'climbed Ben Bulben's back', which he describes in *The Celtic Twilight* as 'famous for hawks', and his footnote to 'Meditations in Time of Civil War' is immediately relevant:

> I suppose that I must have put hawks into the fourth stanza because I have a ring with a hawk and a butterfly upon it, to symbolize the straight road of logic, and so of mechanism, and the crooked road of intuition: 'For wisdom is a butterfly and not a gloomy bird of prey'.— 1928.[2]

It is 'The intellectual gyre' that is growing 'wider and more wide'. We are told in *A Vision*: 'As Christ was the *primary* (objective) revelation to an *antithetical* (subjective) age, He that is to come will be the *antithetical* revelation to a *primary* age.'[3] And again: 'When our historical era approaches . . . the beginning of a new era, the *antithetical* East will beget upon the *primary* West and the child or era so born will be *antithetical*.'[4] The 'gloomy bird of prey' has slipped its leashes, and will soon be lost to sight. In this first verse-draft Yeats follows a symbolic reference with a more topical and specific one: 'the germans are (   ) now to Russia come'. By the end of July 1917 the Russian front had crumbled in face of the enemy. In October of that year the Bolsheviks brought off their revolution, and at the Treaty of Brest-Litovsk, on 3 March 1918, Lenin had surrendered to the Germans: Finland, Esthonia, Courland, Lithuania, and tracts of Russian Poland. The Germans had

[1] Ellmann, *The Identity of Yeats*, 1954, p. 258.   [2] *Variorum*, p. 827.
[3] 1925 edition, p. 169.   [4] 1937 edition, p. 257.

indeed come to Russia, and I think it not impossible that Yeats, with his reverence for the aristocratic virtues epitomized by Castiglione, had in mind the fate of the Russian Royal House, as he wrote: 'Though every day some innocent has died'.

The poem's second verse-draft, after some preliminary scribbles, reads:

F. 2r: ~~Broader & broader is the~~

~~Forth~~

~~ever more wide~~
                                            day by day
                            The gyres sweep wider ~~by year~~
                                            every ~~year~~ day
                            can no more hear the falconer
                            The hawk, ~~flies from the falconer's hand~~
                                    Things have begun to break & f
                            All ~~things are broken up~~ & fall apart

~~After they have got the (   )~~

Then a line or two more of illegible jottings, followed by:

The tyrant has the anarch in his pay

And murderer to follow murderer

Written sideways, across the horizontal lines of F. 1v a stanza begins to take shape:

Things fall apart—at every stroke of the clock

~~*Of innocence most foully put to death*~~

                                    have
~~*Old wisdom and young innocence has died*~~

~~*The gracious and the innocent have*~~

~~*Or*~~ *while the mobs fawn upon the murderer*

And the judge nods before the empty dock.

F. 3r suggests that Yeats was now thinking of anarchy and unrest nearer home than Russia. Again he writes across the horizontal lines:

All things break up—no stroke upon the clock

But ceremonious innocence has died,
    ~~*Yet the*~~ *where*
~~*While*~~ *the mob fawns upon the murderer*
    And
~~*While*~~ *the judge nods before his county dock,*

~~*And there's no Burke to cry aloud no Pitt*~~

And there is none to pluck them by the gown

This last line is written in pencil. On F. 4*r* the first full draft of the poem begins:

                widening gyre
Turning and turning in the wide gyre

The falcon cannot hear the falconer

~~*(   ) the gyres*~~

~~*Things fall apart—the centre has lost*~~
            (   )
Things fall apart—the centre cannot hold
    Mere
~~*Vile*~~ *anarchy is loose there on the world*
    dim tide
The blood stained flood is loose & anarchy

The ceremony of innocence is drowned.
           ~~*intensity*~~
~~*The good are wavering & intensity*~~
    lack   ~~*while*~~
The best ~~*lose*~~ *all conviction while the worst*

Are full of passionate intensity.
    ~~*Surely the great falcon must come*~~
~~*Surely the hour of the second birth is here*~~

~~*We have the desert—say to (   )*~~
    ~~*say (   )*~~
~~*The second Birth! Scarce have those*~~
            words been spoken

Already German and Russian, Burke and Pitt, mob and murderer, and the judge before his dock have fallen away. The poem's scope and focus have widened. Lest particular details distract the reader's eye and limit his vision, Yeats introduces more general terms, such as 'anarchy', 'the ceremony of innocence', 'the good', and 'the worst'. Except for a hint of assonance in the first four lines, rhyme also has been abandoned, for the reason perhaps that it too might distract and limit the reader's attention. The hawk has finally become the falcon, and not only, I suspect, because the metre demanded a disyllable. Had he used hawk, readers versed in his symbolism would have been tempted to make the simple equation, hawk = logic + intellect. Once so clearly defined, a symbol is drained of much of its imaginative potency: but no sooner does he change it to the less familiar falcon, than he injects it with new energy in the form of half-realized associations. Like 'Herodiade's address to some Sibyl who is her nurse, and, it may be, the moon also', Yeats's falcon is the pride of the intellect, and, it may be, more also. There remains, however, a difficulty. 'Surely the great falcon must come' has been crossed out, but we must consider how it came there in the first place. It would seem that for one moment at least, the poet planned to introduce the visionary second coming with 'a gloomy bird of prey'. A passage, previously quoted, from *A Vision* supports this: 'When our historical era approaches . . . the beginning of a new era, the *antithetical* East will beget upon the *primary* West and the child or era so born will be *antithetical*.' It is well known that Yeats saw history as a pattern of recurrent cycles. For him, Leda and the swan that was Zeus had inaugurated one such cycle; Virgin and the dove that was the Holy Ghost had inaugurated another. In the line which he later cancelled, he was saying, I suggest, that the predatory falcon would inaugurate this third cycle. He would then have cancelled it because his symbols were becoming confused. The falcon represents the out-going power, out of which a new antithetical power must be born: as such it cannot fulfil a new annunciation.

F. 5*r* continues the first full draft:

> *Surely some revelation is at hand*
>
> ~~*We have the desert*~~ (   )

must leap
The cradle at Bethlehem has rocked anew
    the second coming is at
Surely the hour of the second birth has struck
    Scarcely are these words
        coming   have   spoken
The second Birth. Scarce have the words been spoken
    and new intensity rent as it were cloth
Before the dark was cut as with a knife
    lost
And a stark image out of spiritus mundi

Troubles my sight. A waste of sand
        —A waste of desert sand
A shape with lion's body & with (   )
        and the head of a man breast & head
Move with a slow slouching step
    A gaze
An eye blank and pitiless as the sun

Slouches   thighs

Moves its slow feet while all about its head

An angry crowd of desert b
    Run
Fall shadows of the desert birds they
        indignant desert birds

On this sheet again we see the poet weeding out particular detail: the over-localized striking of the hour of the second coming, the 'knife' and 'cloth' which diminish the image of the darkness torn, 'An eye' altered to 'A gaze', and the—perhaps too human—'feet' altered to 'thighs'. Ellmann is, I think, on the right track when he says that Yeats 'refers to the image as a "shape", and intends the indeterminate label to increase its portentousness, (and) he makes clear that it is, or is like, the Egyptian sphinx, which is male (unlike the Greek sphinx)'. Yeats, in his *Autobiographies*, tells how as a young man, 'there rose before me mental images that I could not control: a desert and a black Titan raising himself up by his two hands from the middle of a heap of ancient ruins'.[1] This suggests a sub-conscious recollection of Shelley's 'Ozymandias':

[1] p. 185.

> . . . Two vast and trunkless legs of stone
> Stand in the desert. . . . Near them, on the sand,
> Half sunk, a shattered visage lies. . . .

Weeks detects a further Shellean source of 'The Second Coming' in 'Prometheus Unbound' (i. lines 625–8):[1]

> The good want power, but to weep barren tears.
> The powerful goodness want; worse need for them.
> The wise want love; and those who love want wisdom;
> And all best things are thus confused to ill.

Yeats himself says in a note to *Wheels and Butterflies*, that from about 1903 he was always imagining 'at my left side just out of the range of sight, a brazen winged beast that I associated with laughing, ecstatic destruction . . . afterwards described in my poem "The Second Coming" '.[2]

F. 6r concludes the first full draft:

> *The darkness drops again but now I know*

Four lines of illegible scribble, then:

> *That   of its stony*
> ~~*For*~~ *twenty centuries a stony sleep*
>
> ~~*Were vexed & all but broken by the second*~~
> *Were vexed*
> ~~*Were vexed*~~ *to night mare by a rocking cradle*
>
> ~~*And now at last, (   )*~~
>
> ~~*It slouches towards Bethlehem to be born*~~
>
> *It has set out for Bethlehem to be born*
> ~~*that*~~
> ~~*And now at last   knowing its hour come round*~~
>
> *It has set out for Bethlehem to be born*
> ~~*wild thing*~~ *its hour come round at last*
> *And what* ~~*at last*~~ *knowing the hour* ~~*come round*~~
> *rough beast*
> ~~*Is slouching*~~ *towards Bethlehem to be born*
>
> *Slouches towards Bethlehem to be born*[3]

[1] 'Image and Idea in Yeats's "The Second Coming", *P.M.L.A.* lxiii, pp. 281–92.

[2] 1934, p. 103.

[3] On F. 6v is a manuscript draft of 'Michael Robartes and the Dancer', beginning: 'Lady turn from all opinions'.

Inexorably we watch Yeats's pen pursuing the poem's magnificent and sinister conclusion.

The two manuscript fair-copies of 'The Second Coming' are the same as for the first printing, except for punctuation and also in what appears to be the later of the two, it is not 'thirty' but 'twenty centuries of stony sleep'. Miss M. Rudd reveals the phrase 'stony sleep' to have been borrowed (no doubt unconsciously) from Blake's lines in 'The First Book of Urizen':[1]

> Ages and ages roll'd over him
> In stony sleep ages roll'd over him.

At the second printing Yeats changed the iambic pattern of line 13 for the striking, dune-like undulation of 'somewhere in sands of the desert'.

Considering now the completed poem as an artistic whole, we find that most common Yeatsian pattern of an objective first movement passing into a more subjective second movement. There is a natural division between lines 8 and 9, like that dividing the octave of a Petrarchan sonnet from the sestet. Incantatory repetition prepares us for the change:

> Surely some revelation is at hand;
> Surely the Second Coming is at hand.
> The Second Coming!

The prophet comes into the open: 'a vast image. . . . Troubles my sight:'. Having described the image he sums up:

> but now I know
> That twenty centuries of stony sleep
> Were vexed to nightmare by a rocking cradle,

Just as Yeats never wrote a love poem that does not treat of lover as well as of beloved, we are not allowed to overlook the figure of the prophet behind the prophecy.

Only two or three months elapsed between the writing of 'The Second Coming' and 'A Prayer for my Daughter', and not for nothing did Yeats have them printed next to each other. Both, it will be seen, stem from a mood of depression brought on by the First World War, although, in both, references to the conflict are

---

[1] *Divided Image*, 1953, p. 119.

made less explicit in the manuscript drafts. The two poems have also a 'cradle' and a theme in common. 'The ceremony of innocence is drowned' is an idea explored at greater length in 'A Prayer for my Daughter':

> How but in custom and in ceremony
> Are innocence and beauty born?

II

A PRAYER FOR MY DAUGHTER

1. Once more the storm is howling, and half hid
2. Under this cradle-hood and coverlid
3. My child sleeps on. There is no obstacle
4. But Gregory's wood and one bare hill
5. Whereby the haystack- and roof-levelling wind,
6. Bred on the Atlantic, can be stayed;
7. And for an hour I have walked and prayed
8. Because of the great gloom that is in my mind.

9. I have walked and prayed for this young child an hour
10. And heard the sea-wind scream upon the tower,
11. And under the arches of the bridge, and scream
12. In the elms above the flooded stream;
13. Imagining in excited reverie
14. That the future years had come,
15. Dancing to a frenzied drum,
16. Out of the murderous innocence of the sea.

17. May she be granted beauty and yet not
18. Beauty to make a stranger's eye distraught,
19. Or hers before a looking-glass, for such,
20. Being made beautiful overmuch,
21. Consider beauty a sufficient end,
22. Lose natural kindness and maybe
23. The heart-revealing intimacy
24. That chooses right, and never find a friend.

25. Helen being chosen found life flat and dull
26. And later had much trouble from a fool,

27. While that great Queen, that rose out of the spray,
28. Being fatherless could have her way
29. Yet chose a bandy-leggèd smith for man.
30. It's certain that fine women eat
31. A crazy salad with their meat
32. Whereby the Horn of Plenty is undone.

33. In courtesy I'd have her chiefly learned;
34. Hearts are not had as a gift but hearts are earned
35. By those that are not entirely beautiful;
36. Yet many, that have played the fool
37. For beauty's very self, has charm made wise,
38. And many a poor man that has roved,
39. Loved and thought himself beloved,
40. From a glad kindness cannot take his eyes:

41. May she become a flourishing hidden tree
42. That all her thoughts may like the linnet be,
43. And have no business but dispensing round
44. Their magnanimities of sound,
45. Nor but in merriment begin a chase,
46. Nor but in merriment a quarrel.
47. O may she live like some green laurel
48. Rooted in one dear perpetual place.

49. My mind, because the minds that I have loved,
50. The sort of beauty that I have approved,
51. Prosper but little, has dried up of late,
52. Yet knows that to be choked with hate
53. May well be of all evil chances chief.
54. If there's no hatred in a mind
55. Assault and battery of the wind
56. Can never tear the linnet from the leaf.

57. An intellectual hatred is the worst,
58. So let her think opinions are accursed.
59. Have I not seen the loveliest woman born
60. Out of the mouth of Plenty's horn,

61. Because of her opinionated mind
62. Barter that horn and every good
63. By quiet natures understood
64. For an old bellows full of angry wind?

65. Considering that, all hatred driven hence,
66. The soul recovers radical innocence
67. And learns at last that it is self-delighting,
68. Self-appeasing, self-affrighting,
69. And that its own sweet will is Heaven's will;
70. She can, though every face should scowl
71. And every windy quarter howl
72. Or every bellows burst, be happy still.

73. And may her bridegroom bring her to a house
74. Where all's accustomed, ceremonious;
75. For arrogance and hatred are the wares
76. Peddled in the thoroughfares.
77. How but in custom and in ceremony
78. Are innocence and beauty born?
79. Ceremony's a name for the rich horn,
80. And custom for the spreading laurel tree.

YEATS'S daughter Anne was born on 26 February 1919. If we are to believe a cancelled manuscript reference to 'my month-old child', the poem was probably written, or at least begun, in March or April. It was first published in *Poetry*, November 1919.

There are seven loose-leaf sheets of manuscript working, which at the time of composition were in a notebook: and these it has been possible to place in their original order by means of matching the ink-blots. It would seem that Yeats wrote his preliminary rough drafts, as well as a few late corrections, in blue ink, and an intermediate full draft in an ink that has now faded to brown. As there are rough drafts of stanzas II, X, XI, and XII only, I think it probable that these caused him more trouble than the others, and that rough drafts of stanzas I and III–IX existed, but have been destroyed. I have endeavoured to make my transcriptions more intelligible by representing brown ink in ordinary italic and blue ink in bold italic.

F. 1*r* contains part of a fair copy of 'Michael Robartes and the Dancer'. I have seen no early draft of stanza I of 'A Prayer for my Daughter', but on F. 1*v* stanza II begins to take shape:

God grant my prayer

Nor am I the first father that has stood
           here
And judged ~~the~~ here beside this cradle hood
      ~~seeing~~ thinking that
And ~~seeing that~~ a popular tempest blew
                all
As though to make things a ~~knew~~ new,

~~According to opinion, driven men wild~~

~~Decides that some (~~——————~~)~~*

As this opinion wound, had driven men wild

And filled their hearts with bitterness

~~*Feared for this child unless*~~

~~*For Had fear*~~

Had dread for this child's peace unless

Heaven pour abounding sweetness on the child

Under this he begins again:

be
And it may another father stood
                    that
And gazed upon a head below ~~this~~ hood

And thinking what a popular tempest blew

~~*That all things*~~

And thinks if all men's minds anew
       ~~*That*~~
~~*And*~~ *all must be with opinion driven wild*

And full of dusty bitterness

Shuddered for that child's peace unless

These stanzas he crossed out with a diagonal line, and, it would seem, passed to F. 2v on which there are two further drafts, one early and one late. The lower and earlier reads:

II
~~*It may be that soon*~~
Considering that this cradle old may be
                    had like
Some other father has ~~had like~~ reverie

When the wind rose, I thought (   ) bless

Until all things were made anew

All must be with opinion driven wild
       choked with
And ~~full of~~ dusty bitterness

peace
Trembling| ~~*And shuddered*~~ *for his child's* ~~*play*~~ *unless*

Heaven pour abounding sweetness on his child.

The repetition of 'opinion' and 'bitterness' suggests that stanza II
at this stage contained the seed of what was eventually to be
stanza VIII: Yeats was already thinking of Maud Gonne.

I believe that at this point he continued with the rough draft of
the poem, but as there remain only the workings of the last stanzas,
I pass to F. 2r and the start of the full draft. At this stage there is
no title.

I

In her three hundred year old cradle hid

By its deep hood & broidered coverlid

My month-old child is sleeping & today

Her laughter proved her heart to be gay
        because the times are ~~*for*~~ *ever has*
While I ~~*that have been indifferent long must cast*~~
        My sight towards every ~~*scowling*~~ *howling quarter.*
        ~~*My gaze my sight towards every scowling quarter*~~
~~*A scrupulous gaze on every quarter*~~

My sight towards ever howling quarter
        To   ~~*blows wind*~~ *blast has*
~~*And*~~ *judge what* ~~*wind has*~~ *heaven charted*
        What is some demagogue's song
~~*To level all things, what*~~ *is bellows-blast*

II

Nor am I| ~~*I am not*~~ *the first father that has*
~~*Many another father may have stood*~~
        ~~*Where   And weighed (   )*~~
~~*As I stand now beside*~~ *this cradle-hood*

Time| *And judged by the* ~~*blast*~~ *beside*

And as all times have trouble, this own
        the world fell
Thought the ~~*storm beaten*~~ *stone upon stone*

> *and that the masters of the world ran*
> ~~*The world fell while its masters had*~~ *gone wild*
>
> *And racked his brain to think of all*
>
> *That might that sleeping child befall*
> ~~*And what were the best prayer to pray for the*~~
> ~~*And prayed as I some charmed gift for his child*~~
>
> *And what to ask of heaven for the child*
>
> ~~*And what prayer might be best*~~

These two stanzas have been crossed out with diagonal lines. On F. 2v is a later draft:

> *storm*
> *Once more the ~~wind~~ is howling & half hid*
>
> *Under the cradle hood & coverlid*
>
> ~~*My child sleeps on but on western*~~ *hill*
>
> *My child sleeps on—There is no obstacle*
>
> *But Gregory's wood & one bare hill*
>
> *Where by the haystack & roof levelling wind*
>
> *Bred on the Atlantic can be checked.*
>
> *Not by that storm am I perplexed*
>
> *But by the storm that seems to shake mankind*

Already the detail of the cradle's great age has fallen away. Though interesting, it directs the reader's attention to the cradle rather than to the child. In its place, and heightening the contrast with the sleeping child, he introduces more details of the storm. Violence and tranquillity are in constant opposition throughout this poem. The lines:

> ~~*The world fell while its masters had*~~ *gone wild*

and:

> *Not by that storm am I perplexed*
>
> *But by the storm that seems to shake mankind*

remind us that the First World War had only recently dragged to its close. Reference to this cataclysm again distracts attention from the central theme, and it too is abandoned. For the third stanza, with its veiled allusion to Maud Gonne, we must turn back to F. *2r*:

III

> *I pray God grant her beauty &*
> ~~*Beauty enough I pray her*~~ *& yet not*
>
> *Beauty to make a stranger's eye distraught*
>
> *Or hers before a looking glass for such*
>
> *Being made beautiful overmuch*
>
> *Consider beauty a sufficient end*
>
> *Lose natural kindness & maybe*
>
> *The heart revealing intimacy*
>
> *That chooses right & never finds a friend*

From Maud Gonne his mind moves naturally to the doom-laden beauties of antiquity. F. *3r* continues this draft:

IV

> *Helen being chosen found life flat & dull*
>
> *And later had much trouble from a fool*
>
> *While that great queen that rose out of the spray*
>
> *Being fatherless could have her way*
>
> *Yet chose a bandy legged smith for man*
>   *It's certain that fine women*
> ~~*So it is plain great beauties*~~ *eat*
>
> ~~*Some crazy (   ) amidst*~~
>
> *A crazy salad with their meat*

D

> gather
> ~~Nor find a better till all days are run~~
>
> ~~That never should in wholesome sun~~
>   *Whereby great plenty's horn is half undone*

Historical and legendary exempla lead him to a lesson that he had himself learnt by bitter experience.

V

> ~~Chiefly in   I have her deeply~~
> ~~But in all courtesy I would have her learned~~
>
> *In courtesy I'd have her chiefly learned*
>
> *Hearts are not had as a gift but hearts are earned*
>
> *By those that are but partly beautiful*
>
> *Yet many that has played the fool*
>
> *For beauty's very self has charm made wise*
>
> *And many a poor man that has roved*
>
> *Loved & thought himself beloved*
>   *a*
> ~~That~~ *from   glad kindness cannot take his eyes*

VI

> ~~Grant her an even temper & good health~~
>   *O let her live contented as a bird—*
> ~~Grant her a quiet manner & good health~~
>   *That in the left hand bush a moment heard*
> ~~A husband children & a little wealth~~
>   *A moment later in the right hand sings*
> ~~Yet not enough for joys that have no part~~
>   *Nor can in all its travelled*
> ~~In the self delighting heart~~
>
> *On that, ~~all~~ when eyes upon a promised face*
>
> *With present faces quarrel*
>
> *O let her live like some green laurel*
>
> *That is rooted in one dear, perpetual place.*

In classical mythology, of course, Daphne, daughter of the river-god Peneus, was metamorphosed into a laurel tree which subsequently became the favourite of Apollo. F. A. C. Wilson suggests that here, as in the last stanza of 'Among School Children', the tree is a symbol for Unity of Being. Yeats asks, in effect, that his daughter may become 'a living image of the (Kabbalistic) Tree of Life'.[1] This version of stanza VI he crossed out with a single line, and we see him trying again as he begins F. *4r*:

VI

O let her live contented as a bird

That in the left hand bush a moment heard

A moment later on the right hand sings

And will not though it clap its wings

For the excitement of an unknown face

With customary faces quarrel

Or let her live like a green laurel

Rooted in one dear perpetual place.

VII

Because those causes I have most approved

And certain things & people I have loved

Have prospered little my own mind of late

Has grown half barren from much hate

stet   *I* ~~therefore~~ *pray one gift | of all gifts chief |* ~~that is~~

Hatred| ~~For hate~~ *once driven from the mind*

That bird need never toss in the wind

Or that green leaf become a yellow leaf;

[1] *Yeats's Iconography*, 1960, p. 303.

These stanzas VI and VII have also been crossed out, and at the
right-hand side of each is written 'see back'. I therefore insert here
the corrected stanzas from F. 4*v*:

~~Make her a hidden fruitful flowering tree~~

May she become a flourishing hidden tree
     become
~~May she grow up a pleasant flourishing tree~~

That all her thoughts may like the linnet be

And have no business but dispensing round

Their magnanimities of sound

Nor but in merriment begin a chase

Nor but in merriment a quarrel

O may she live like some green laurel

Rooted in one dear perpetual place.

Has lost its foliage from much hate

I therefore pray this gift, of all gifts chief

Banish ~~all hatred from~~ her mind   hate out of |

That ~~she gone she~~ may fear the wind   never|

Nor that green leaf become a yellow leaf

The above fragment from stanza VII has been scored out, and
beneath it is the finished text of that stanza (with the exception of
only the most minor alterations):

My mind because the minds that I have loved

The sort of beauty that I have approved

Prospers but little has dried up of late;[1]

Yet knows that to be choked with hate

[1] . . . but little . . . is in red ink.

May well be of all evil chances chief.

If there is no hatred in a mind

Assault & battery of the wind

Can never tear the linnet from the leaf.

We return now to F. *4r* and a more obvious reference to Maud Gonne:

VIII

> *Seeing that hate is*
> ~~*And*~~ *intellectual* ~~*hatred is the*~~ *worst*
> $\qquad\qquad$ *be*
> *Let her think all opinions* ~~*are*~~ *accurst*
>
> *O I have seen the loveliest woman born*
>
> *Out of the mouth of plenty's horn*
>
> *Because of her opinionated mind*
>
> *Barter that horn & every good*
>
> *By quiet natures understood*
>
> *For an old bellows full of angry wind*

IX

> *Considering that all hatred driven hence*
> $\qquad\qquad$ *recovers its radical*
> *The soul* ~~*draws near its first*~~ *innocence*
>
> *And learns at last that it is self delighting*
>
> *Self appeasing, self affrighting*
>
> *And that its own sweet will is heaven's will*
>
> *She can, though every face should scowl*
>
> *And every windy quarter howl*
>
> *Or every bellows burst be happy still.*

Although Yeats at this point almost certainly passed on to the full-draft version of stanza X on F. 5*r*, I shall here break off to consider the rough workings of three stanzas that were never to find their way into print. I shall examine later the reasons for the rejection of this finale. On F. 6*v* Yeats would seem to have turned the notebook upside down and scribbled a thirteen-line prose draft. Of this I am able to read little more than the recurrent word *daughter*. Then, turning the notebook the right way up again, he wrote on F. 5*v*:

> If that you are happy daughter & yet grown
>
> ~~Daughter~~ if you be happy | & yet grown
>
> Say when you are four & 20 walk alone
>   on an October day
> Through Coole domain, ~~upon a summer's~~
>
> ~~Or when~~
>
> ~~When the last~~
>
> ~~When all the equinoxial gales~~
>   has
> Or when new summer parched the hay
>
> ~~Or when the latest lingering storm~~
>
> ~~Or when the l~~
>
> Or when the lingering winter has ~~gone~~ gone
>
> ~~Or~~ aye or upon what day you please
>
> If there's no roaring in the trees
>
> ~~Daughter &~~
>   you
> And ~~you~~ are happy daughter—yet grown
>
> ~~If but you~~
>
> And under the

Cancelling this page with a diagonal line, Yeats returned to F. 6*v* and wrote—this time the right way up:

My daughter if when you have grown you find
when   if you
~~If you have grown up daughter & yet find~~

The horn of plenty not the flighty wind

Walk up to Coole on some October day

Or when the summer's parched the hay

Or at the end of the spring equinox

Aye or upon what day you please

If there's no roaring in the trees

Nor splashing at the hollow of the rocks

Here, for the moment, he leaves stanza X, and on F. 6r begins on a stanza XI:

And ramble there ~~alone beside~~ the lake
*   a little by the lake*

~~And by walk~~

~~Visit the stony edges of the lake~~

Where I have counted swans, & for my sake

If you are ~~happy daughter & yet grown~~

~~And st~~ *Standing upon a lofty arch alone*

~~Stand on a lake encircled stone~~
*   If that you are happy daughter & yet grown*
Cry out that all is well ~~till all~~ until that cry

Travels the lake, & all that's there

Spring sounding upon the still air

And all is sound between the lake & sky.

Dissatisfied with this, he recasts the stanza below:

Then where what light the beach boughs can let through

Cannot make green what ivy has made blue

~~Speak it again but in~~

Speak these same words again, but in such tone
    that you
If ~~you~~ are happy & yet grown

~~As will not~~   as can scarce man

~~Then there's no need to raise your voice~~
    (   ) need at all
If: ~~no~~ need ~~at all~~ to raise your voice

If that you do not make a noise

~~By climbing thither at too brisk a place~~ pace
    ~~By~~
~~Climbing~~ climbing upwards at too brisk a pace

On F. 4v there is a later, and better, version of stanza XI:

Then at the lovely hour when a star's light

Or that of the blanched moon has leaped to sight

Although the bitter daylight be not gone
            unquiet
If you are happy & yet grown

Call from Stand at the garden at the western side

Near the Katalpa tree & call

Until the echo in the wall

Above Maecenas' image has replied.

The only rough draft of stanza XII is on F. 7v, written rapidly
aslant the page:

Nor think that being dead I cannot hear
  Or   I cannot if god will
~~Nor~~ that ~~god willing I may not~~ appear
              alive
Among those places that ~~alive~~ I loved
  Motionless   at   or
~~Standing to think by~~ lake ~~or~~ wood

>   *upon a*
> *Or hurry thought driven ~~on a~~ vaporous foot*
>
> *Where for some twenty years or so*
>   *paced*
> *My friend & I ~~walked~~ to & ~~fro~~ fro*
>
> *Upon the gravel by the Katalpa root.*

I now return to F. 5*r* and the full-draft of these three stanzas:

X

> *Daughter be happy & yet grown—*
>
> *Say when you are five & twenty—walk alone*
>
> *Through Coole Domain & visit for my sake*
>
> *The stony edges of the lake,*
>
> *Where every year I have counted swans, & cry*
>
> ~~*That all is well but cry it not*~~
>
> ~~*Aloud that all is well but cry it not*~~
>
> ~~*Too loud for that is a still spot*~~
>
> *That all is well till all that's there*
>
> *Spring sounding on to the still air*
>
> *And all is sound between the lake & sky*

XI

>   *beach foliage can*
> *Then where what light ~~the tall beach boughs~~ let through*
>
> *Falls green on ground the ivy has made blue*
>
> *Cry out that all is well but cry it not*
>
> *Too loud for that is a still spot*
>   ~~*And after to the garden on that*~~   *And after to the garden*
> ~~*Then to the garden on its southern side*~~   *on that side*
>
> *Where the Katalpa's grow & call*   *growing/*

Until an echo in the wall

Above Mæcenas' image has replied.

XII

What matters it if you be overheard

By gardener, labourer or herd

They must that have strong eye-sight meet my shade

When the evening light's begun to fade

Amid the scenery it has held most dear

Till many a winter has gone by.

No common man will mock the cry

Nor think that being dead I cannot hear

April 1919.

Stanza XII has been crossed out, and an arrow points down the page to these lines:

Nor think that being dead I cannot hear

~~Because it is certain that for many a year~~

~~For it is certain~~ that I shall appear

If you have perfect sight

Standing to think where I have often stood

By the lake's edge, in that blue wood

~~On the short path by the Katalpa root~~

path

Where the ~~rock~~ climbs between a rock & root

Or ~~where~~ else, where twenty year or so

My friend & I paced to & fro

Hungry though driven on a vaporous foot,

F. 5*r* is dated April 1919, but the typescript carries the date June
1919. Between these dates considerable changes were made, but
as I have seen no manuscripts of this period through which to plot
the poem's progress, I can only make comparison with the typescript[1] and the printed text.

In these the first stanza has been pruned of detail. Cradle's age,
child's age, and the broidery on the coverlid have gone. The
theme is now stated with simplicity and dignity:

> And for an hour I have walked and prayed
> Because of the great gloom that is in my mind.

Repetition at the start of the second stanza emphasizes the point:
'I have walked and prayed for this young child an hour', and the
movement of the verse suggests the backward and forward pacing
of Yeats himself on the top of Thoor Ballylee. All reference to
earlier fathers has been cast out, to sharpen the focus yet further.
The gloom and terror of the moment is now brilliantly conveyed
in the description of the storm:

> I have walked and prayed for this young child an hour
> And heard the sea-wind scream upon the tower,
> And under the arches of the bridge, and scream
> In the elms above the flooded stream;

In the repetition of 'scream' we catch the rising hysteria of the
wind, which leads in the second half of the stanza to the wider
vision of approaching cosmic violence:

> Imagining in excited reverie
> That the future years had come,
> Dancing to a frenzied drum
> Out of the murderous innocence of the sea.

The one significant alteration in stanza III is the omission of
the direct reference to God. Yeats is careful not to commit himself

[1] The only significant variants in the typescript are:
  Line 4. But Gregory's Woods . . .
    18. Beauty as to make . . .
    21. Consider beauty as sufficient end,
    35. By those that are beautiful not entirely; (error?)
    36. Yet many that has played the fool
    65–72 are missing. I can only think this is a typist's error, as the stanza exists in
      the manuscript drafts.
    73. And may she marry into some old house

to orthodoxy, and begins the stanza: 'May she be granted beauty'. Stanzas IV, V, VI, and VII differ little in the printed version from the manuscript. VIII receives new vigour when direct statement becomes rhetorical question: 'Have I not seen the loveliest woman born . . . ?'

As I have already suggested, the great change in the poem's direction comes in its finale. The first-written stanza X echoes the poem 'The Wild Swans at Coole', which although written in 1917, was published by Macmillan's on 2 March 1919—in fact, while 'A Prayer for my Daughter' was being composed. What with proof-reading and press reactions, the earlier poem might be expected at this moment to be at the forefront of Yeats's mind. In the first version of the 1919 poem, the prayer for Anne Yeats brings the poet's thought round to:

> her that took
> All till my youth was gone
> With scarce a pitying look.

All roads lead to Maud Gonne, and it is a movement off course when he allows his memory to side-track him into recollections of Coole Park and Lady Gregory ('my friend'). We find reference to the Catalpa tree (spelt correctly) in a later poem, also about Coole and its inmates, entitled 'The New Faces'. The image of Maecenas, patron and protector of Virgil and Horace, was appropriately placed in Lady Gregory's garden.

In the first-written stanzas X, XI, and XII, Anne simply provides an excuse for Yeats to talk about himself. He, not his daughter, is at this stage the true subject of the poem. His sharply self-critical eye, however, must have perceived that the divided emphasis halved the impact of the poem: the three stanzas were cut out, and one new one grafted in their place:

> And may her bridegroom bring her to a house
> Where all's accustomed, ceremonious;
> For arrogance and hatred are the wares
> Peddled in the thoroughfares.
> How but in custom and in ceremony
> Are innocence and beauty born?
> Ceremony's a name for the rich horn
> And custom for the spreading laurel tree.

This brilliantly preserves the poem's balance, and ties into a single knot the themes of arrogance and hatred (with their plebeian overtones suggested by 'peddled' and 'thoroughfares'); and aristocratic custom and ceremony. The overall rhetorical structure is now impeccable. Not without a struggle, Yeats had remained true to his original intention: he had written a prayer, not for himself, but for his daughter and, on another level of interpretation, for the world.

III

THE SORROW OF LOVE

1. The brawling of a sparrow in the eaves,
2. The brilliant moon and all the milky sky,
3. And all that famous harmony of leaves,
4. Had blotted out man's image and his cry.

5. A girl arose that had red mournful lips
6. And seemed the greatness of the world in tears,
7. Doomed like Odysseus and the labouring ships
8. And proud as Priam murdered with his peers;

9. Arose, and on the instant clamorous eaves,
10. A climbing moon upon an empty sky,
11. And all that lamentation of the leaves,
12. Could but compose man's image and his cry.

YEATS'S post-publication revisions of his early poetry have for long been a skirmishing ground between an Old Brigade of critics, who, on the whole, regretted them, and a New Brigade, who did not. As is the way with such encounters, the New Brigade seem to have had the best of it. There remains only one pocket of resistance; over 'The Sorrow of Love' the Old Guard make their last stand. Most recently, G. B. Saul, in his *Prolegomena to the Study of Yeats's Poems*, made an uncharacteristic confusion between fact and opinion, when he stated that the earlier versions 'were inherently more logical and less pretentious, and hence more charming'. Although Louis Macneice also holds this view,[1] R. Stamm makes a good case for saying 'that Yeats knew very well what he was doing when he changed the early version';[2] but no one, I think, has yet fully appreciated the extent and subtlety of his changes.

Ellmann gives us the manuscript version of the poem,[3] which was written in October 1891.

> *The quarrel of the sparrows in the eaves,*
>
> *The full round moon and the star-laden sky,*
>
> *The song of the ever-singing leaves,*
>
> *Had hushed away earth's old and weary cry.*
>
> *And then you came with those red mournful lips,*
>
> *And with you came the whole of the world's tears,*
>
> *And all the sorrows of her labouring ships,*
>
> *And all the burden of her million years.*

[1] *The Poetry of W. B. Yeats*, 1941, pp. 69–72.
[2] *English Studies*, xxix, pp. 79–87.
[3] *The Identity of Yeats*, 1954, p. 317.

And now the angry sparrows in the eaves,

The withered moon, the white stars in the sky,

The wearisome loud chanting of the leaves,

Are shaken with earth's old and weary cry.

Before its first printed appearance, in *The Countess Kathleen and Various Legends and Lyrics*, Yeats had made certain alterations. Lines 3 and 4 became:

And the loud song of the ever-singing leaves
Had hid away earth's old and weary cry.

In line 8, 'million' was changed to 'myriad'; in line 9, 'angry sparrows' to 'sparrows warring'; in line 10, 'withered moon' to 'crumbling moon'; and line 11—'The wearisome loud chanting of the leaves' to 'And the loud chanting of the unquiet leaves'. 'The Sorrow of Love', as it stands at this stage in its development, is an almost perfect expression of the prevailing Pre-Raphaelite mood of the 1890's. Both its diction and its subject suggest the influence of Pater's celebrated description of *La Gioconda*:

Hers is the head upon which all "the ends of the world are come," and the eyelids are a little weary. It is a beauty wrought out from within upon the flesh. . . . All the thoughts and experience of the world have etched and moulded there, in that which they have of power to refine and make expressive the outward form, the animalism of Greece, the lust of Rome, the reverie of the middle ages. . . .

Of this Yeats speaks in his introduction to *The Oxford Book of Modern Verse*, and chose to open his selection with a passage from it, written out in the form of free verse.

Saul finds the earlier versions of 'The Sorrow of Love' 'more logical and less pretentious'. There is, however, an illogicality in the manuscript version which is not fully corrected in the published version of 1892. 'Sparrows', 'moon', 'sky', and 'The song of the ever-singing leaves' are first said to have 'hushed away earth's old and weary cry'. Moon and sky are clearly incapable of hushing anything; probably for this reason Yeats altered 'hushed' to 'hid'. This is a move in the right direction, but not even the verb 'hide'

can apply equally to a visual moon and sky, and the sound of
sparrows and ever-singing leaves. 'Earth's old and weary cry'
seems to me a highly pretentious phrase. The poet means, I think,
what Matthew Arnold called 'the eternal note of sadness', but seeks
to compensate for a lack of precise meaning by a somewhat facile
resonance.

In early versions of the second stanza Yeats addresses himself
directly to Maud Gonne: 'And then you came with those red
mournful lips'. Macneice comments: 'The mood is piled up with
hyperboles (poetic clichés)—"the *whole* of the world's tears", "*all*
the sorrows", "*all* the burden", "*myriad* years".' It is in the nature
of hyperbole—'the over-reacher', as Puttenham called it—to be
pretentious. It must pretend to be more than it is, but to be effective it must deceive the reader into acceptance. Yeats's hyperbole
is not fully successful because there seems to be no logical reason
why the woman should have been attended by 'all the sorrows' of
the world's 'labouring ships'. Tears may perhaps suggest the sea,
but I have an irreverent suspicion that it was the demon rhyme
who suggested that 'ships' should follow 'lips'. Stamm in a good
footnote says: 'those "red lips" appear in other poems as part of
Yeats's imagery of dangerous beauty: cf. the beginning of *The
Wanderings of Oisin* where the hero and his fellows meet

> A pearl-pale, high-born lady, who rode
> On a horse with bridle of findrinny;
> And like a sunset were her lips,
> A stormy sunset on doomed ships;'

This last is a striking image, and has an internal logic not to be
found in the 1892 version of 'The Sorrow of Love', where the
intimate 'you' is not strong enough to support the weight of
hyperbole.

'The full round moon' of stanza I has become in stanza III
'The withered', and later, 'The crumbling moon'. What at first
sight appeared to be a record of instant revelation admits the
presence of time, and at once something of the intensity of the
experience is dissipated.

The illogicality of stanza I is repeated in stanza III. 'Sparrows', 'moon', and 'stars' may be 'shaken with earth's old and weary cry', but not 'the loud chanting of the unquiet leaves'. 'Shake' might be considered too physical a verb to perform at the same time a literal and a figurative function. 'Earth's old and weary cry' (which, I suspect, caused the poet to abandon the earlier epithet 'wearisome'), being still unexplained, is unsatisfactory. For all the lyrical beauty of the earlier versions—and the polysyndeton of the second stanza I find especially effective—Yeats has not yet brought his subject into focus. The emotional colour is there, but the intellectual outlines are everywhere indistinct.

'The Sorrow of Love' that, in its final form, appeared first in *Early Poems and Stories* (1925), startled and perplexed many for whom the original version was an established favourite. The first alteration they would have noticed was itself slight, but typical of the more radical structural changes to come. 'The quarrel of the sparrows' was now more sharply defined as, 'The brawling of a sparrow'. Parkinson, I think, quibbles unnecessarily when he questions whether one sparrow can brawl, for, as he himself goes on to say: 'The change from "quarrel" to "brawling" gives more vigour to the sparrow's cry, suggests by antithesis the "cry" of man in the closing line of the revised stanza, and makes that cry more harsh.' Not only is the ear arrested by the more forceful verb (which incidentally anticipates 'The emperor's brawling soldiers', in an early draft of 'Byzantium'), but the mind's eye now seizes on the single sparrow.

A major alteration appears in the two references to the moon. Yeats himself is not altogether correct when he says:

here and there in correcting my early poems I have introduced . . . numbness and dullness, turned for instance, 'the curd-pale moon' into the 'brilliant moon', that all might seem, as it were, remembered with indifference, except some one vivid image.

'The full round moon' (of line 2) he had altered to 'The brilliant moon'; and 'The curd-pale moon' (of line 10) to 'The climbing moon'. This change of epithets becomes more significant when we remember that Yeats in 1925 had only recently completed his chapter on the phases of the moon for *A Vision*. In the poem

entitled 'The Phases of the Moon' (1918) he had already echoed
'The Sorrow of Love' in the line: 'And after that the crumbling
of the moon'. By 1925 a 'full round moon' meant to Yeats the
fifteenth phase of pure subjectivity, and lest the new wine burst
the old bottle, he altered the epithet to 'brilliant'. Even more
important is the fact that 'brilliant' and 'climbing' can refer now
to the same phase of the moon. Between stanzas I and III there is
no longer a time-lag, and the poem records a single moment of
revelation.

Of the change in line 3, whereby 'The loud song of the ever-
singing leaves' became 'And all that famous harmony of leaves,'
Saul says that 'that famous harmony' 'seems readable merely as a
deliberate phrase, without esoteric reference'. This should imply
no criticism, because 'that'—even if spurious—cunningly recalls
the 'ille' of the Latin epic, and prepares for the classical imagery
of the second stanza. 'Harmony' suggests a pattern seen as well as
heard, so that the sight of 'The brawling sparrow', 'moon', 'sky',
and 'leaves' can be said to have 'blotted out man's image', and the
musical 'harmony of leaves' to have blotted out man's cry. Macneice wrote of the 1892 version: 'the poem is all of a piece. It is
clear what it is about—Nature set over against the troubles of
humanity.' Surely this is much clearer in the final version. 'Man's
image and his cry' is more easily interpreted as the troubles of
humanity than is 'earth's old and weary cry'.

The most important alteration in the poem is in the increased
objectivity of line 5: 'A girl arose that had red mournful lips'.
She is now larger than life: Maud Gonne has been merged in Eve,
Deidre, Helen—the eternal figure of the tragic heroine. Where an
identifiable personality could not support the weight of hyperbole,
a symbol can. Yeats had already shown his dissatisfaction with
lines 7 and 8 by altering them in 1899 to:

> And all the trouble of her labouring ships
> And all the trouble of her myriad years.

Not until *The Green Helmet and Other Poems* (1910) did he discover
the full potency of the Helen symbol. In writing the final version of
'The Sorrow of Love' he was able to give the poem a new level of

association, and (I submit, for the first time) make full sense of lines 7 and 8. The girl is now:

> Doomed like Odysseus and the labouring ships
> And proud as Priam murdered with his peers.

Another Helen is in tears at the realization of her handiwork—Odysseus doomed and Priam murdered. Something of the situation's tragic inevitability is conveyed in the slow drum-beat of the alliterating consonants.

Just as between stanzas I and II the image of the moon, with all its traditional associations of flux and feminine inconstancy, gave place to the image of the tragedy-queen's face, so between stanzas II and III the sequence is reversed. In both cases the transition is as subtle as that of Sir Philip Sidney's lament, in which he sees himself reflected in the moon:

> With how sad steps, O moon, thou climbst the skies!
> How silently and with how wan a face!

The initial 'Arose' of stanza III picks up that in line 5, and hurries the verse movement on. The girl 'arose' and the moon 'climbing' show their single identity. As the moon's face had suggested to the poet the face of his beloved, proud though doomed, dignified but certain to wane, so the noise of the leaves would seem to have suggested 'the world in tears'.

The poem at last records a single experience, whose outline—faithfully followed by the outline of the verse—is firm and clear. The troubling image of the girl dispels the first enchantment and serenity: 'on the instant' eaves are clamorous, the moon climbing, and the leaves lamenting: together they 'Could but compose man's image and his cry'. The bitter fact of the sorrow of love has shattered the dream of peace. The sky, formerly 'milky', is now 'empty'. The first epithet may well have been prompted by a conscious or subconscious recollection of Tintoretto's famous picture, 'The Origin of the Milky Way'; and there would seem in this change from 'milky' to 'empty' more than an overtone of feminine sterility. Whereas in its early versions the poem ended inconclusively with 'earth's old and weary cry' coming from nowhere to shake the sparrows, moon, sky, and leaves, the last line, as revised in 1925, clinches the poem.

By 1925 Yeats had long since put off his Pre-Raphaelite spectacles, and could look back at himself with a more searching objectivity. Not until then did he finish his poem, and for that reason I have not discussed it earlier. Perhaps Yeats should be allowed to have the last word himself: 'Whatever changes I have made are but an attempt to express better what I thought and felt when I was a very young man.'[1]

[1] Notes to *Early Poems and Stories*, 1925, p. 528.

IV

THE GIFT OF HARUN AL-RASHID

1. Kusta Ben Luka is my name, I write
2. To Abd Al-Rabban; fellow-roysterer once,
3. Now the good Caliph's learned Treasurer,
4. And for no ear but his.
                              Carry this letter
5. Through the great gallery of the Treasure House
6. Where banners of the Caliphs hang, night-coloured
7. But brilliant as the night's embroidery,
8. And wait war's music; pass the little gallery;
9. Pass books of learning from Byzantium
10. Written in gold upon a purple stain,
11. And pause at last, I was about to say,
12. At the great book of Sappho's song; but no,
13. For should you leave my letter there, a boy's
14. Love-lorn, indifferent hands might come upon it
15. And let it fall unnoticed to the floor.
16. Pause at the Treatise of Parmenides
17. And hide it there, for Caliphs to world's end
18. Must keep that perfect, as they keep her song,
19. So great its fame.
                        When fitting time has passed
20. The parchment will disclose to some learned man
21. A mystery that else had found no chronicler
22. But the wild Bedouin. Though I approve
23. Those wanderers that welcomed in their tents
24. What great Harun Al-Rashid, occupied

25. With Persian embassy or Grecian war,
26. Must needs neglect, I cannot hide the truth
27. That wandering in a desert, featureless
28. As air under a wing, can give birds' wit.
29. In after time they will speak much of me
30. And speak but fantasy. Recall the year
31. When our beloved Caliph put to death
32. His Vizir Jaffer for an unknown reason:
33. 'If but the shirt upon my body knew it
34. I'd tear it off and throw it in the fire.'
35. That speech was all that the town knew, but he
36. Seemed for a while to have grown young again;
37. Seemed so on purpose, muttered Jaffer's friends,
38. That none might know that he was conscience-struck—
39. But that's a traitor's thought. Enough for me
40. That in the early summer of the year
41. The mightiest of the princes of the world
42. Came to the least considered of his courtiers;
43. Sat down upon the fountain's marble edge,
44. One hand amid the goldfish in the pool;
45. And thereupon a colloquy took place
46. That I commend to all the chroniclers
47. To show how violent great hearts can lose
48. Their bitterness and find the honeycomb.

49. 'I have brought a slender bride into the house;
50. You know the saying, "Change the bride with spring,"
51. And she and I, being sunk in happiness,
52. Cannot endure to think you tread these paths,
53. When evening stirs the jasmine bough, and yet
54. Are brideless.'

               'I am falling into years.'

55. 'But such as you and I do not seem old
56. Like men who live by habit. Every day
57. I ride with falcon to the river's edge
58. Or carry the ringed mail upon my back,

59. Or court a woman; neither enemy,
60. Game-bird, nor woman does the same thing twice;
61. And so a hunter carries in the eye
62. A mimicry of youth. Can poet's thought
63. That springs from body and in body falls
64. Like this pure jet, now lost amid blue sky,
65. Now bathing lily leaf and fish's scale,
66. Be mimicry?'
                     'What matter if our souls
67. Are nearer to the surface of the body
68. Than souls that start no game and turn no rhyme!
69. The soul's own youth and not the body's youth
70. Shows through our lineaments. My candle's bright,
71. My lantern is too loyal not to show
72. That it was made in your great father's reign.'

73. 'And yet the jasmine season warms our blood.'

74. 'Great prince, forgive the freedom of my speech:
75. You think that love has seasons, and you think
76. That if the spring bear off what the spring gave
77. The heart need suffer no defeat; but I
78. Who have accepted the Byzantine faith,
79. That seems unnatural to Arabian minds,
80. Think when I choose a bride I choose for ever;
81. And if her eye should not grow bright for mine
82. Or brighten only for some younger eye,
83. My heart could never turn from daily ruin,
84. Nor find a remedy.'
                     'But what if I
85. Have lit upon a woman who so shares
86. Your thirst for those old crabbed mysteries,
87. So strains to look beyond our life, an eye
88. That never knew that strain would scarce seem bright,
89. And yet herself can seem youth's very fountain,
90. Being all brimmed with life?'
                     'Were it but true
91. I would have found the best that life can give,

92. Companionship in those mysterious things
93. That make a man's soul or a woman's soul
94. Itself and not some other soul.'

                                        'That love
95. Must needs be in this life and in what follows
96. Unchanging and at peace, and it is right
97. Every philosopher should praise that love.
98. But I being none can praise its opposite.
99. It makes my passion stronger but to think
100. Like passion stirs the peacock and his mate,
101. The wild stag and the doe; that mouth to mouth
102. Is a man's mockery of the changeless soul.'

103. And thereupon his bounty gave what now
104. Can shake more blossom from autumnal chill
105. Than all my bursting springtime knew. A girl
106. Perched in some window of her mother's house
107. Had watched my daily passage to and fro;
108. Had heard impossible history of my past;
109. Imagined some impossible history
110. Lived at my side; thought time's disfiguring touch
111. Gave but more reason for a woman's care.
112. Yet was it love of me, or was it love
113. Of the stark mystery that has dazed my sight,
114. Perplexed her fantasy and planned her care?
115. Or did the torchlight of that mystery
116. Pick out my features in such light and shade
117. Two contemplating passions chose one theme
118. Through sheer bewilderment? She had not paced
119. The garden paths, nor counted up the rooms,
120. Before she had spread a book upon her knees
121. And asked about the pictures or the text;
122. And often those first days I saw her stare
123. On old dry writing in a learned tongue,
124. On old dry faggots that could never please
125. The extravagance of spring; or move a hand
126. As if that writing or the figured page

127. Were some dear cheek.
                                    Upon a moonless night
128. I sat where I could watch her sleeping form,
129. And wrote by candle-light; but her form moved,
130. And fearing that my light disturbed her sleep
131. I rose that I might screen it with a cloth.
132. I heard her voice, 'Turn that I may expound
133. What's bowed your shoulder and made pale your cheek';
134. And saw her sitting upright on the bed;
135. Or was it she that spoke or some great Djinn?
136. I say that a Djinn spoke. A livelong hour
137. She seemed the learned man and I the child;
138. Truths without father came, truths that no book
139. Of all the uncounted books that I have read,
140. Nor thought out of her mind or mine begot,
141. Self-born, high-born, and solitary truths,
142. Those terrible implacable straight lines
143. Drawn through the wandering vegetative dream,
144. Even those truths that when my bones are dust
145. Must drive the Arabian host.
                                    The voice grew still,
146. And she lay down upon her bed and slept,
147. But woke at the first gleam of day, rose up
148. And swept the house and sang about her work
149. In childish ignorance of all that passed.
150. A dozen nights of natural sleep, and then
151. When the full moon swam to its greatest height
152. She rose, and with her eyes shut fast in sleep
153. Walked through the house. Unnoticed and unfelt
154. I wrapped her in a hooded cloak, and she,
155. Half running, dropped at the first ridge of the desert
156. And there marked out those emblems on the sand
157. That day by day I study and marvel at,
158. With her white finger. I led her home asleep
159. And once again she rose and swept the house
160. In childish ignorance of all that passed.
161. Even to-day, after some seven years

162. When maybe thrice in every moon her mouth
163. Murmured the wisdom of the desert Djinns,
164. She keeps that ignorance, nor has she now
165. That first unnatural interest in my books.
166. It seems enough that I am there; and yet,
167. Old fellow-student, whose most patient ear
168. Heard all the anxiety of my passionate youth,
169. It seems I must buy knowledge with my peace.
170. What if she lose her ignorance and so
171. Dream that I love her only for the voice,
172. That every gift and every word of praise
173. Is but a payment for that midnight voice
174. That is to age what milk is to a child?
175. Were she to lose her love, because she had lost
176. Her confidence in mine, or even lose
177. Its first simplicity, love, voice and all,
178. All my fine feathers would be plucked away
179. And I left shivering. The voice has drawn
180. A quality of wisdom from her love's
181. Particular quality. The signs and shapes;
182. All those abstractions that you fancied were
183. From the great Treatise of Parmenides;
184. All, all those gyres and cubes and midnight things
185. Are but a new expression of her body
186. Drunk with the bitter sweetness of her youth.
187. And now my utmost mystery is out.
188. A woman's beauty is a storm-tossed banner;
189. Under it wisdom stands, and I alone—
190. Of all Arabia's lovers I alone—
191. Nor dazzled by the embroidery, nor lost
192. In the confusion of its night-dark folds,
193. Can hear the armed man speak.

THIS poem has always been something of a mystery, for neither style nor setting link it with any other poem that Yeats ever wrote. It is neither concerned with old Irish myth nor modern Irish martyrs. On the surface its subject is Arabic, but although Owen Aherne is alleged to have supplied the story, neither he nor Robartes features in it.

Few of the critics have advanced very far into the labyrinth. T. R. Henn suggests that, 'it owes much, in structure and rhythm, to Browning's "Karshish" '.[1] From Yeats's letters we know that he had read and re-read Browning, but considered him 'a dangerous influence'. Certainly the opening of Browning's Epistle suggests that of Yeats's poem:

> Karshish, the picker-up of learning's crumbs . . .
> To Abib, all-sagacious in our art.

Thereafter, although the two epistles have a theme in common with which I shall deal later, their styles are so different that I cannot believe that Yeats was indebted to 'Karshish'. His primary source is much more obvious, and none other than the tales of *The Thousand and One Nights*, so many of which centre around the Khalifat Haroun Al-Rachid.

Mrs. Yeats tells me that her husband 'learnt his Arabic' from Sir Edward Denison Ross,[2] who may well have introduced him to the *Arabian Nights*. Certainly he must have been acquainted with them before writing the Preface to *A Vision* (1925), in which he says: '. . . for the moment my imagination dwells upon a copy of Powys Mathers' "Arabian Nights" that awaits my return home. I would forget the wisdom of the East and remember its grossness and its romance.' The sixteen volumes of this translation were privately printed by the Casanova Society. Bodley's copy is stamped September 1923, which is not too late to have been a

---

[1] *The Lonely Tower*, 1950, p. 48.

[2] Sometime director of the School of Oriental Studies and professor of Persian in the University of London; he died in 1940.

source for 'The Gift of Harun Al-Rashid', which Yeats dated simply 1923.

Many of Shahrazade's tales, as I said earlier, are concerned with the adventures of the Khalifat Haroun Al-Rachid. 'The Tale of Beauty-Spot'[1] is the most relevant to Yeats's poem; not as the source of the epistle, but as the source of a play from which I believe the poem is derived. The play is James Elroy Flecker's *Hassan*, which was published posthumously in 1922, the year before Yeats wrote 'The Gift of Harun Al-Rashid'. Before I go further I must say that Mrs. Yeats does not support my theory. Her husband, she says, hated Flecker's work and had not read *Hassan* before writing his poem. I am sure Mrs. Yeats is right, that Yeats, as an old man, must have hated Flecker's sugary Oriental lyricism, but we must remember that the 'modern' poet of 1939 was a Pre-Raphaelite in his youth. There is, in fact, evidence that at one time Yeats *did* like Flecker's work. In a monograph by T. S. Mercer is quoted a letter from James Elroy to his father: 'Do you realize that your son is thought by Gosse, Yeats, Gilbert Murray and also, thank God, by some editors to be far the greatest poet of his day, barring Yeats?'[2] Again, Douglas Goldring in his biography of Flecker quotes a letter written in 1914, in which the poet says: 'Seems I've lost the Polignac prize, damn it. Murray and Yeats voted for me. Damn everything.'[3] Flecker died on 3 January 1915, when Yeats's poetic style had only recently undergone its metamorphosis. His sympathy with Flecker's romantic manner was bound to wear thin as he himself moved farther away from it, but he nevertheless included three of Flecker's poems in *The Oxford Book of Modern Verse*.

The tale of Beauty-Spot has several points of resemblance to *Hassan*. An impotent Syndic buys himself a virility potion, as a result of which his wife gives birth to handsome Aladdin Beauty-Spot. The Khalifat Haroun Al-Rachid one night walks about the streets of Baghdad in disguise, with his Wazir Giafar (the Vizir Jaffer); Masrur, the sworder; and his poet Abu Nowas. Beauty-

---

[1] *The Book of the Thousand Nights and One Night*, translated by E. Powys Mathers, 1923, Book V, p. 144.

[2] *James Elroy Flecker, from School to Samarkand*, 1952, p. 44.

[3] *James Elroy Flecker, an Appreciation*, 1922, p. 120.

Spot becomes a favourite of the Khalifat, and in the market he buys the lovely slave Yasmine for 10,000 dinars as his second wife. In the course of a complicated tale of jealousy, involving the Khalifat's Chief of Police, Beauty-Spot is convicted of theft; sentenced to death; escapes; is separated from his faithful Yasmine; but at last they are reunited and he recovers the Khalifat's favour.

More ingredients of *Hassan* are to be found in other tales of *The Thousand Nights and One Night*.

Haroun Al-Rachid has his poet Abu Nowas stripped and sentenced to death by Masrur: he is just reprieved in time.[1] There are many mentions of the Khalifat's favourite musician, Abu Ishak.[2] In one of the many tales beginning: 'One night the Khalifat, Haroun Al-Rachid, left his palace, accompanied by his wazir Giafar . . .', &c., they are enraptured by a voice singing to the lute, knock on a door, and are shown into a splendid house where a tale is told by Abu Al-Hassan.[3]

On this material as a foundation Flecker built *Hassan*. I believe that Yeats did see it, or read it, before he came to write his poem. Though there would be much in it for him to dislike, there would be much also that might appeal to him: the Eastern setting with 'its grossness and its romance'; the epigrammatic wit so reminiscent of Oscar Wilde and the 90's; the ideal love of Rafi and Pervaneh, culminating, like that of Forgael and Dectora, in death; the ghosts; and finally the poet-figures Hassan and Ishak, who take the golden road to a Samarkand not unlike Yeats's own Byzantium. Whether Yeats liked *Hassan* or not, I believe he saw in it something that he wanted; a ready-made mythology to fit a personal experience. This was the discovery, made on his honeymoon in 1917, of his wife's automatic writing. As she lay in a state of trance, voices (allegedly) spoke through her, whose philosophic pronouncements Yeats copied out, put into order, and eventually published in *A Vision*.

A prose summary of the story, in its mythological fancy dress, originally accompanied the poem, but was dropped after the fourth printing. One part of it in particular shows us the man behind the mask.

---

[1] E. Powys Mathers, op. cit., Book VI, p. 50.
[2] Ibid., Book VII, p. 126.   [3] Ibid., Book IX, p. 80.

... Kusta, a Christian like the Caliph's own physician, had planned, one version of the story says, to end his days in a monastery at Nisbis, while another story has it that he was deep in a violent love-affair that he had arranged for himself. The only thing upon which there is general agreement is that he was warned by a dream to accept the gift of the Caliph, and that his wife, a few days after the marriage, began to talk in her sleep, and that she told him all those things which he had searched for vainly all his life in the great library of the Caliph, and in the conversation of wise men.[1]

This is autobiography in the thinnest of disguises; indeed, the note was perhaps abandoned because it was so transparent. The suggestion that Kusta might end his days in a monastery means simply that the poet foresaw a celibate old age, dedicated to art and philosophy. The violent love affair can only refer to the frustrated relationships with Maud and Iseult Gonne. Both versions of the story are true; he has just separated the aspirations of soul and body.

The one character not immediately recognizable behind the mythological mask is the Caliph. Who gave Yeats his bride? No man, certainly. The answer can only be some divine power or providence, and the idea for the equation of Deity with Caliph, I believe Yeats found in *Hassan*. Flecker's Harun Al-Raschid speaks of himself as 'The shadow of God on Earth, and Peacock of the World'. Hassan says: 'He is exalted far above Mankind.' The soldiers address him as: 'The Holy, the High-born, the Just One, the Caliph.' These extravagant hyperboles are, of course, not to be taken seriously. Flecker's Caliph shows his nature to be as much compounded of lust and ferocity as that of lesser mortals, in his barbarous treatment of Rafi and Pervaneh. Far from depriving a man of his bride, Yeats's Caliph presents Kusta with one; and yet in line 31 Abd Al-Rabban is reminded that:

> ... our beloved Caliph put to death
> His Vizir Jaffer for an unknown reason:

There is no precedent for this in *Hassan*, so Yeats's authority must be the tale in *The Thousand Nights and One Night* in which Shahrazade tells of the end of Giafar and the Barmacides.[2] 'Giafar was

[1] *Variorum*, p. 828.
[2] E. Powys Mathers, op. cit., Book XVI, p. 161.

the life of Al-Rachid's eyes', until suddenly one night Masur, the sworder, burst in, saying: 'The Commander of the Faithful demands your head from me.' There are given four possible reasons for Giafar's execution:[1]

I. Barmacide extravagance, leading to jealousy in the Khalifat and amongst his courtiers.

II. Giafar's refusal to kill Al-Sayed Yahia bin Abdalla Al-Hossayni, as the Khalifat had commanded.

III. Heretical opinions held in the face of Islamic orthodoxy. The Barmacides had tried to prevent the destruction of the temples of the Magi.

IV. Complications arising from Giafar's marriage to the Khalifat's sister, Abbassah, who was his other favourite.

Other and quite worthy historians contend that Giafar and the Barmacides had done nothing to deserve their fate. Whatever the Khalifat's reasons, 'his resentment was stronger than death. He ordered the body to be crucified at one end of the bridge of Baghdad, and the head to be exposed at the other.'[2] Yeats must have been aware of the manner of Giafar's death: I suspect he omitted it from his poem to avoid an over-specific equation of God the Father with the Caliph, and God the Son with Jaffer. Not being himself a Christian, he would have preferred the more general symbol that can fit any 'dying God'. There is a hint of divine regeneration in Yeats's mention that, after the killing, the Caliph, 'Seemed for a while to have grown young again;' 'Jaffer's friends' must be Christ's disciples and the followers of Dionysus, who mourn together in the play The Crucifixion. Browning's poem 'Karshish' and 'The Gift of Harun Al-Rashid' have in common their allusions to the 'dying God'.

It is one of the weaknesses of Yeats's epistle that this introduction is insufficiently related to the central story of Kusta and his wife, which begins:

> The mightiest of the princes of the world
> Came to the least considered of his courtiers;
> Sat down upon the fountain's marble edge,

[1] E. Powys Mathers, op. cit., Book XVI, pp. 168–80.   [2] Ibid., p. 166.

In their balanced antithesis and alliteration these lines are pure
Flecker. The 'beautiful fountain, with the silver dolphin and the
naked boy' is referred to at least half a dozen times in *Hassan*. It
could even be one of the clustered associations behind one of
Yeats's most powerful symbols:

> Straddling each a dolphin's back
> And steadied by a fin
> These innocents relive their death,

The Hassan–Yasmin relationship is radically altered in Yeats's
poem. The old poetical confectioner's love for the beautiful harlot,
he alters to fit the facts of experience; but the magical name Yasmin
lingers on, albeit in a European rather than an Arabic spelling:

> When evening stirs the jasmine bough . . .

> And yet the jasmine season warms our blood.

Yeats's symbolic use of the first and fifteenth phases of the moon is
consistent with the theories of *A Vision*, but his ear may well have
been arrested by Yasmin's words to Hassan:

> When the bird of night sings on the bough of the tree that rustles
> outside your window, and the shadows creep away from the moon
> across the floor, I could have sung you a song sweeter than the nightin-
> gales, and shown you a whiteness whiter than the moon.

Departing for a moment from 'The Gift of Harun Al-Rashid', I
believe there are echoes of Flecker in some of Yeats's other poems.
The Caliph's line: 'Let me study the hatred in his eyes', may have
prompted Ribh's: 'I study hatred with great diligence'. Pervaneh's
talk of: 'The trumpets of Reality that drown the vain din of the
Thing that Seems', may be echoed by a line in 'Vacillation': 'The
Soul. Seek out reality, leave things that seem'. Finally—though this
comes close to heresy—the most famous line in Yeats's 'Byzantium': 'That dolphin-torn, that gong-tormented sea.' could be an
unconscious development of two lines from Flecker: first, one
from *Hassan*: 'Across that angry or that glimmering sea.' and
secondly, one from 'The Gates of Damascus': 'The dragon-green,
the luminous, the dark, the serpent-haunted sea.'

Having investigated the probable sources of Yeats's poem, we
come now to the manner in which it was composed. The earliest

draft that I have seen is written untidily, and with a thick, freely flowing nib, on ten loose-leaf sheets. For the most part he has written on only one side of the page—the right, as it would have been in the notebook—but there are occasional corrections scribbled on the left. Crossings out are many and heavy, and so fast did Yeats cover the pages that he frequently smudged them when he turned over.

F. 1r: ~~Place~~

> Lets
>
>   Treasure
> (Old friend & fellow student) ~~lay~~ these lines
>
> ~~By~~
>
> ~~Somewhere in the old library that boards~~
>
> ~~On~~
>
> ~~The rose garden~~
>   un
> Somewhere in this old little unfrequented house
>
> ~~That hold~~
>
> ~~That hides the rose garden from the desert sands~~
>
> ~~That the guards the garden from the desert~~ winds
>   Hide this away
> Where your chief treasures ~~are ; find it a place~~
>
> ~~Near Sappho's manuscript~~
>   Near to   all
> ~~Beside~~ some manuscript ~~no coming age the coming age~~
>
> ~~With (————————————)~~ coming & time
>
> ~~Must guard from worm,~~
>   ~~Must guard~~   worm
> Must guard from ~~worm worm,~~ or sacriligious hand
>
> ~~Ever it may be~~
>
> ~~Ever it may be~~
>
> ~~Old~~

Ever it

Ever it may,

Ever it may be —
     Aye   friendship can so far forgive what seems
Ever, if you can forgive what seems

Presumption, by that great book of Sappho's song

For I describe a mystery mystery they would not
                                        have
For they desire a mystery, & would they would learn

The wandering Arab for sole chronicler.

'Old friend & fellow student' is so familiar an opening that I
cannot help wondering whether Yeats had not someone definite
in mind, when he began his epistle. This would seem to be supported by the reference to: '. . . this old little unfrequented house.
. . . Where your chief treasures are;'. Already, however, we can
see him moving from the familiar to the impersonal and dignified:

     Aye   friendship can so far forgive what seems
Ever, if you can forgive what seems

Presumption, . . .

He also alters 'For I describe a mystery' to the more objective 'For
they desire a mystery'. F. 2r carries on directly from F. 1:

They have read my thought

There

The shadow of my thought

They have taken to their heads the thought

Those
                                        dream
Those that have welcomed in their tents, the thought

That our beloved lord, sole

That our great lord, sole emblem upon earth

~~Of Providence~~
    The Beloved
~~Our great~~ *Haroon Er-Rasheed, occupied*

~~With all~~

~~With~~

~~With all the state office~~

~~With all~~

With the great toil & ceremony of state

Must needs neglect, to those I am most grateful

I cannot hide the truth. Much wandering

Through the great desert that is featureless
     Even
~~Even~~ *as the air has given*
    ~~As~~
~~Even as the air gives this~~ *a bird wits.*

Yeats crossed these lines out, before continuing below:

In after time they will speak much of me

And speak but lies.

                    it all
     But you shall know ~~all the truth~~

~~How (   ) thoughts that yet may change the last~~

~~How that which I have saught from childhood up~~

~~Has been revenged~~

We two are fallen into years though vigorous yet.

We two at at the most in twenty years

The dream, which the Arabs welcome and the Caliph of Baghdad ('sole emblem upon earth Of Providence') neglects,

. . . refers to the geometrical forms which Robartes describes the Jud-wali Arabs as making upon the sand for the instruction of their young

people, & which, according to tradition, were drawn as described in
sleep by the wife of Kusta-ben-Luka.[1]

That the Caliph-Deity has neglected this philosophical system—
being too 'occupied With the great toil & ceremony of state'—
I take to be Yeats's explanation for the absence of his 'system' from
all previous religious teachings.

F. *3r* continues:

~~All of my life, that is set upon the parchment~~

~~Only that little portion of our thought~~

~~That is upon the parchment, or remembered~~

~~Or half remembered by an ageing friend~~

~~All~~

We shall be but that moiety of ourselves

That is upon the parchment, or remembered

~~Or half remembered by~~

~~By mind~~

By ears too busy to remember much

~~Or not to learn~~

~~Or not~~
                        before the embers gone
Or not to find ~~a little before long~~

~~Too great a burden upon this written page~~

~~A wearisome encumbrance hence this parchment.~~

~~Where~~

~~Where is~~

~~Where is it made plane that all I saught~~

~~From childhood up has come to me unsaught~~

---

[1] Yeats's footnote to the poem's first printing in *The Dial*: see *Variorum*, p. 830.

That little an encumbrance—Hence this parchment

Where it is made ~~plane~~ plane that all I saught

From childhood up has come to me unsaught

These tangled reflections on the future of the poet's reputation, and on his past acquisition of wisdom, he properly abandons; for they are an irrelevant digression from his story. At this stage there is no mention of the death of the Vizir Jaffer, and the narrative opens abruptly on F. 4r:

Harroun er Rascheed, the most bountiful

And mighty of the princes of the world
    ~~Call~~ *Came to the*
~~Called for~~ *the least considered of his courtiers*

~~And spoke one hand planted upon the marble edge~~

~~And seated upon the border of his fountain~~
    upon the
Sat down the fountain's marble edge
    One
~~One~~ *hand amid the goldfish in the pool*
*   *began this*
*   *And there upon ~~a~~ colloquy took place*

~~And spoke these memorable words~~

That should be kept in memory to show
    ~~How can can~~
~~That minds that be terrible in anger~~
              this
~~Can be all kindness, "I have brought into the~~ ( ) *house*

Dissatisfied with the two previous lines, he tries again:

*   ~~That even minds that are most terrible~~

*   ~~To private &~~
        ~~can be~~
*   ~~How eyes that have a terrible at need~~

---

  * Indicates a line inserted from the left-hand page (F. 3v) at a point marked by a connecting arrow.

* ~~To private or to public enemy~~

* ~~Cherish a friend servant~~

* ~~Can melt in kindness "when the spring~~

* ~~Cherish a friend "when the first jessamine flowered~~
*   have
* I brought a slender bride into the house
          new tall slender
    ~~A new tall bride into the house~~
          You   change
    ~~They~~ know the saying change the bride with spring

~~Though you that are as changeless as they say~~

(————)
     ~~Must hold~~
And she & I being lost in happiness

~~Cannot endure~~

~~Are saddened~~

Cannot endure to think you tread those paths
     ~~As the evening~~ evening
~~Where the~~ when ~~evening~~ stirs the jessamine & yet

Are brideless"

          —   "I have

               "I have fallen into years"

~~He said~~

On F. 5*r* the Caliph replies:

~~And there upon my master~~
          ~~Master~~
Nor have the first down my cheek
                         seem
Men such as you & I do not ~~grow~~ old

Like men who live by habit—every day

~~Some new (————) body~~

               * See note at foot of opposite page.

I ride the hawk upon a rist, or ~~(———)~~ *hand*

~~Or or~~

~~Or~~

~~To chase~~

~~Upon the desert (——————)~~

~~Or carry the ringed mail upon my back~~

S

~~I follow~~

~~I rise the game out of the riverbank~~ *river*
    Or
~~I~~ *ride with falcon to the river's edge*
    I
~~Or~~ *carry the ringed mail upon my back*

Or chase a woman ~~(———)~~ ~~enemy~~ ~~(———)~~ ~~enemy~~

Yeats's Deity here exhibits some of the characteristics of the Olympian Zeus, who 'Accomplished his predestined will' on Leda and Europa.

~~Nor game nor woman~~

Nor   ~~& there is not one~~
           ~~no armed enemy~~
           & never enemy
Game bird, or woman does the same thing twice.

~~You have your thought made every day~~ *& never*

~~Rising out of sense~~

You have your thought that rises every day

~~From sense~~

~~From (———)~~

From ~~your~~ *body as this fountain springs*

Out of its pool, ~~& sinks again~~

F. 6r: ~~In body, & makes body live anew~~

~~being an artist's thought~~

~~After making~~

~~And sinks in body again, &~~

We hunters have a hawk's look in the eye
~~To~~ That imitates our youth;
~~That keeps you us young — you have~~ an artist's thought
      springs
~~That That from body sinks in body again~~

~~The springs up from the body every day~~
                out of   and   in
~~As this clear that~~ spring ~~from~~ body ~~falls into the~~ body falls

~~As this clear musical spring scattering jet~~

~~Springs from its pool, & sinks in body again~~

~~As~~

~~And after sinks after to the green weed & foliage (   )~~

~~And then sinks down into source —~~

~~As this there~~

~~Like that clear~~

~~Like this clear spring scatter~~

~~Like this clear jet that seems~~

Like this pure jet, now lost amid blue sky
        lily leaf or
Now bathing ~~the green weed &~~ fish's scale;
    that
And is youth itself.

The Caliph-Deity, of course, is 'changeless', and so, he says, is the 'artist's thought' as it rises and falls like the fountain beside them. Kusta Ben Luka replies:

All though our souls

Are nearer to the surface of the ~~body~~ body

~~Than other souls that~~
    ~~Than that this~~
~~Than souls never rhymed or started game~~

~~It~~

F. 7r: *Than souls, that start no game & turn no rhyme*

It the soul's & not the body's ~~yo~~ youth

That moulds the lineament.

                        Yet you & I

To take our pleasure when the spring comes round

Yeats, I suspect, meant the Caliph to say: 'Yet you & I Can take our pleasure'. Kusta continues:

                                        my
Great prince forgive the freedom of ~~speech~~ speech

~~But you can let the spring carry away~~
            ~~brought~~
~~What the spring while I that hold~~

(——————), ~~what~~

~~If spring should carry off what the spring brought~~

~~You would not think it too unnatural~~

~~If spring should carry off what the spring brought~~

~~Whereas, seeing that I hold the western Faith,~~

~~And think~~

~~I think~~

~~Whereas I, holding to that western faith~~

~~That seems too unnatural to eastern eyes~~

On the left-hand F. 6v he finds the words he has been groping for,
and expresses the opposition of east and west in a manner more in
keeping with his story:

> ~~But could~~
>
> ~~You think that love has seasons I expect~~
>
> You think that love has seasons; & you think
>
> The spring may carry off what the spring brought
>
> Yet ~~yet~~ see it all without a pang; but I
>
> Who have accepted the Byzantine faith
>
> That seems unnatural ~~in~~ ^{to} Arabian ~~eyes,~~ minds,
>
> Think when I choose a bride I choose for ever.
>
> ~~And (   )~~
>
> ~~And I would feel~~
>
> ~~And so would feel, if her two younger~~ eyes
>
> ~~And so would feel, if eyes that~~
>   And if her eye should not grow bright for mine
> ~~And so if eyes, that had dear me once~~
>   Or   at some younger eye
> ~~Should~~ brighten only ~~for some younger man's~~
>
> ~~I'd know the defeat~~
>
> I'd know the pang of ~~that~~ ^a defeat.

Yeats returns to F. 7r for the Caliph's reply:

>   But what
>
> If I have found a woman that so ~~loves st~~ shares
>
> ~~The toil that has filled your~~
>
> ~~The hope that has disquieted your life~~
>
> ~~I hope~~

The longing that disquiets all your life

~~The power the mystery, the belief~~

       see

~~The~~ To ~~pierce~~ beyond our life, ~~this young eye~~

F. 8r: *~~That love~~*

                          An eye

~~That never strained to~~

           never

That ~~has never~~ known that strain ~~could~~ would scan the length.

~~And yet~~

~~And yet her self seems youth~~

And yet herself can seem youth's very fountain

So rammed is she with life.

'Rammed' is a strong word, but it bears no relevance to 'youth's very fountain', and before its first printing Yeats altered the line to read: 'Being so brimmed with life'. Kusta Ben Luka answers:

                        could

              If this ~~can~~ be

~~The best that lives can be companionship~~

~~In those mysterious things that make a man~~

I would have found the best that life can give

Companionship in those mysterious things

~~That a man himself & not some other~~

That make a man's soul or a woman's soul

Itself & not some other soul

The Caliph's final speech confirms his allegiance to the body rather than the soul:

                    Such ~~a~~ love

~~Must needs herself be changeless here~~

Must needs in life, & when this life has past

Be changeless, & yet

Be changeless & changeless & brings peace on the spirit

Be changeless & at peace & it is right

Philosophers should love such

Philosophers should value more that love

These lines, which were finally to crystallize as:

> That love
> Must needs be in this life and in what follows
> Unchanging and at peace, . . .

bear an interesting and significant resemblance to the opening of 'The Dancer at Cruachan and Cro-Patrick'. Someone, who is obviously Old Tom, says of someone else, who is just as obviously the Unknown God:

> I, proclaiming that there is
> Among birds or beasts or men
> One that is perfect or at peace,
> Danced on Cruachan's windy plain,

On F. 9r the Caliph continues on the subject of philosophers:

But I being none am different

I love to think

My passion deapens
           passion stronger
It makes my passion strong but to think
      Like
Like passion stirs the peacock & his mate mate

The doe & stag, &

The wild deer & the stag and that to kiss

Is man's

Is a man's man's mockery of the changeless soul.

The boar & the wild sow & that to kiss

Is

The wi

The wild stag & the doe, that mouth to mouth

Is a man's mockery of the changeless soul."

That was the first speech of her that now
                the beginning of the joy
And that was my first news of her that now

Is my delight & comfort—she had seen
                the
My passage to court or treasure House

Heard stories of me & invented more

As a girl will, &

These lines Yeats emends on the left-hand F. 8*v*:

And that was the beginning of a joy
The   autumnal chill
That brings more blossom to *my fading years*
    That bursting
Than *all that* spring time knew; for she it seems

Perched in some window of her mother's house
    Pondered
Had seen my daily progress to the court;

There is nothing in this manuscript to correspond with lines 110–87 of the finished text, for F. 10*r* is a draft of the poem's last six lines:

The beauty of a woman's mind, or body

* *A woman's beauty, her love's quality*
*   a tall   of silk
* *Is but a banner of silk or or golden thread*
                        heavy
    Or   Is an embroidered, *or a,* golden banner

* *Or furled with ivory & silver cordes*

* Denotes a line written in green crayon.

~~And it stands a~~

~~And under it stands the leader of the horde~~

~~And under~~

~~And under it armed wisdom stands, but I~~

~~I only of all living~~ men

~~One man out of this thousand ignorant years~~

Under it armed wisdom stands, but I ~~alone~~ have had

~~Only I~~ I only in ten thousand ignorant years

~~I only in ten thousand ignorant years~~

~~Not blinded by the gold, nor drugged by the wind~~

~~That swings the embroidery know had a voice~~

~~And know~~

Not blind with gold, nor drugged with wind

That swings the embroidery, the ~~wisdom s~~ wisdom speak

Here then is a problem: did the poem at its first draft contain no account of the young bride's automatic writing? I cannot believe this to be the case, for the missing lines are as central to the narrative as a mainspring to a watch, and without some description of the phenomenon the dramatic metaphor of the closing lines is 'sound and fury, signifying nothing'. Bearing in mind such poems written shortly after his marriage as 'Solomon to Sheba' and 'On Woman', it is not surprising to find the germ of the metaphor in *The Song of Solomon* (chap. vi, v. 4): 'Thou art beautiful, O my love, as Tirzah, comely as Jerusalem, terrible as an army with banners.'

I think it is quite possible that Yeats wrote this poem in two parts, roughly corresponding with a picture and its frame. There would seem to be a natural division between his experience and the surrounding allegory, and it may be that the missing 'picture' was drawn at another time and subsequently lost. It is more simple, perhaps, to suppose that pages have been lost from the present manuscript; and until they are recovered we must not altogether reject the possibility that F. 10 *did* originally follow F. 9.

I have seen no further manuscript drafts of the poem in this early stage, but prior to its first printing there were at least two stages of typescript. Of the first, F. 6 (lines 114–36) alone remains, and will be considered later. The second typescript, with its one carbon copy, is nine sheets long and has corrections in ink like those for the first printing, but they, except for the last sheet, are too minor to merit independent scrutiny. I pass therefore to the text of the poem that was printed in *English Life and The Illustrated Review*, in January 1924. The Caliph's name was spelt in the manuscript draft, Haroon Er-Rasheed, and becomes in the poem's first title:

The Gift of Haroun El Rashid

Kusta Ben Luki is my name, I write
For the great Calif's treasurer and my friend,
Faristah, and no living ear but his.

Take this light parchment, pass through the great chamber
Where gold-embroidered banners of the Calif's
Await the hour of war, enter the small,
Pass books of learning from Byzantium
Written in gold upon a purple stain,
And pause at last, I was about to say,
At the great book of Sappho's song; but no
If you should hide my parchment in that book
A boy's love-lorn, indifferent hands might find
And it would fall unnoticed on the floor.
Pause at the treatise of Parmenides
And hide it there,

The poem's beginning is here much altered and expanded. The 'Old friend & fellow student' has become 'the great Calif's treasurer and my friend': 'this old little unfrequented house' has become the Caliph's library. It is interesting to see here 'gold-embroidered banners', which clearly anticipate that other gold-embroidered banner at the poem's close. There is again a significant change in Kusta's instructions to his friend: he asks now that the parchment be placed not 'by that great book of Sappho's song', but in 'the treatise of Parmenides'. From this I think we are to infer that his parchment has more in common with the philosophy of Parmenides than with Sappho's love poetry. The long didactic poem written by Parmenides of Elea opens with an allegory describing his chariot journey from the House of Night to that of Day, where he is greeted by a goddess whose welcoming address forms the remainder of the work. The parallel is obvious and surely intentional. Yeats's poem is also an allegory of the progress from darkness into the light of understanding; a progress which, I suggest, is initiated by a divine figure.

On page 70 I noted that the poet's original reflections on the permanence of 'the little portion of our thought That is upon the parchment' had been cut before the poem's first printing. Lines 26–32 (numbering as in the *Variorum*) then read:

> . . . but cannot hide the truth
> Wandering in a desert featureless
> As air under a wing can give birds wit.
> In after time they will speak much of me
> And speak but lies.
> Call up to memory
> That year when great Haroun El Rashid killed
> His Vizier Jaffer for an unknown reason;

The 'wandering Arabs' cannot help but be intelligent since they have to find their way about the featureless desert. It is significant that this somewhat trivial aside is followed, in the 1924 version, by a new paragraph introducing the central narrative with Haroun El Rashid's 'killing' of his Vizier Jaffer. This in the final text is altered to:

> . . . our beloved Caliph put to death
> His Vizir Jaffer for an unknown reason:

I suspect that Yeats changed these lines because the verb 'killed' might be taken to mean that the Caliph in person performed the act: 'put to death' suggests correctly, on both historical and allegorical levels, that he was responsible for the execution.

I have already mentioned the existence of folio 6 of a typescript composed prior to the first printing. It owes its survival, I suspect, to the fact that it includes one of the few passages in the poem

which clearly caused Yeats some trouble: the lines in question are
115–27 (numbering as in the *Variorum*):

> Or did the torchlight of that mystery
>
> Pick out my features in such light and shadow
>
> To contemplating passions chose one theme
>
> Being frenzy struck. Scarce had she trod the floor
>
> Scarce had forgot the strangeness of my presence
>
> Before she had taken down some book and asked
>
> About an emblem or a picture there;
>
> And often those first days I saw her muse
>
> An old dry writing spread upon her knees
>
> In some learned tongue or deep beyond her grasp
>
> And there were moments when she moved as though
>
> Strong hands upon her shoulders made her move
>
> And in that dream she seemed content to touch
>
> As though the written or the pictured page
>
> Were some dear face.

At the first printing this passage reads:

> Or did the torch light of that mystery
> Pick out my features in such light and shade?
> Two contemplating passions chose one theme
> Through sheer bewilderment: she had not paced
> The garden paths nor counted up the rooms,
> Nor had forgot the strangeness of my presence
> Before she had spread a book upon her knees
> And asked about these pictures or those others;
> And often those first days I saw her stare
> On old dry writing in a learned tongue,
> On old dry faggots that could never please
> The extravagance of spring; or certain times

> She moved her limbs confusedly as though
> Hands upon either shoulder made her move,
> And that she dreamed awake content to touch
> As though the written or the pictured page
> Were some dear face.

There is here no important change of substance; but it is interesting to see Yeats cut out the striking compound epithet 'frenzy struck', presumably because he had already used it memorably in the poem 'Beggar to Beggar Cried'. The alteration of 'An old dry writing' to 'On old dry writing' may well have occurred to him as he chanted the line aloud.

The rest of the description of the revelation brought to Kusta Ben Luka by his bride has (as far as line 184) even fewer and slighter changes. Here and there a line is tightened; one (line 154a) is cut, and there are two probable misprints corrected. In line 143 'the wondering vegetative dream' becomes 'the wandering vegetative dream'; and in line 145 'Made drive' (a dictation error for 'May drive'?) becomes 'Must drive'. The actual narrative is self-explanatory, except for the references to the first 'moonless night', and that other, 'When the full moon swam to its greatest height'. Mrs. Yeats's automatic writing had, as its dominant theme, a philosophical system related to the twenty-eight phases of the moon, whose special characteristics are described at length in A Vision. The two phases alluded to here are diametrically opposed to each other, and are respectively phase one (total objectivity) and phase fifteen (total subjectivity). I do not think that in this context Yeats means more than that the young bride's revelation concerned the area between these two extremes.

Lines 187 to the end of the poem, which were heavily corrected in the first draft, underwent further alterations before making their first appearance in print as:

> The beauty of a woman's mind or body
> Is but a heavy, gold embroidered banner,
> Under it armed Wisdom stands, a separate Wisdom
> For every separate quality of love;
> And I alone, one in ten thousand years,
> Not blind with gold, nor dazzled by the gold
> That storms are shaking, hear the armed man speak.

The second corrected typescript, mentioned on page 80, shows
these lines in transition between their first and second printing.
Some alterations have already been incorporated in the typescript:
others have been scribbled between the lines in both ink and
pencil. F. 9 of this typescript begins with line 184:

> *For all those gyres & cubes and*
> ~~Those cones and cubes and gyres, those~~ midnight things,
>
> Are but a new expression of her body
>
> Drunk with the bitter sweetness of her youth.   *N.P.*
> *   *And now my utmost mystery is out*
> *   utmost mystery*
> ~~And now my secret's out, my truth of truths,~~
>
> A woman's beauty is a storm tossed banner;
>
> Under it wisdom stands, / I alone, /   *and/*
>
> *ten/* Out of ~~the~~ thousand winters I alone,
> *   deep*
> Nor dazzled by the embroidery, nor ~~caught~~
>
> ~~Among the folds, can hear the armed man speak~~.
> *In the   its*
> ~~Among~~ confusion of ~~these the~~ night-dark folds
>
> *Can hear the armed ~~man speak~~ man speak*

There is now a more elaborate preparation for the final climax:
'. . . my utmost mystery is out:'. By this the reader's curiosity is
aroused, and it is well sustained through three lines of rhetorical
suspension to the last dramatic trimetre: 'Can hear the armed man
speak.'

There exists, surprisingly, one further fragment of manuscript:
it is a fair copy of lines 1–118 of the poem in its final state, which
the poet may well have prepared for his publisher. There are no
major changes of substance between the poem as first printed in
English Life and the Illustrated Review, and the text first printed in
book form. At its second printing in a magazine there had been
added lines 3, 7, 181, and 192, but at the same time Yeats cut lines

---

* Inserted from the bottom of the page.

18a, 119a, 125a, b, c, 154a, and 189a: he later cut line 25a when preparing the poem for *A Vision* (1925).

Many of Yeats's poems show a sequence, and can be strung as beads on to one string; the early love poems, for example, from *The Wind among the Reeds*, or the Crazy Jane poems, or the Ribh poems. 'The Gift of Harun Al-Rashid', however, has no closer companion than that other blank verse piece, 'The Phases of the Moon', with which it was published in *A Vision*. The two poems were there entitled 'The Wheel and the Phases of the Moon' and 'Desert Geometry or the Gift of Harun Al-Rashid'. As the Caliph is not even mentioned in 'The Wheel and Phases of the Moon', there is little to be gained by comparing the two poems, and we are left with the problem of why Yeats never used the subject of 'The Gift of Harun Al-Rashid' again.

The answer, I think, must be that the poem never fully satisfied him; but why not? Surely because it is an allegory, and his opinion of the respective merits of symbolism and allegory had been formed as far back as 1902 when he wrote the introduction to his selections from the poetry of Spenser. 'I find that though I love symbolism, which is often the only fitting speech for some mystery of disembodied life, I am for the most part bored by allegory, which is made, as Blake says, "by the daughters of memory", and coldly, with no wizard frenzy.' He explores this theme further in his essay 'The Symbolism of Poetry', and there seems to agree with the German Symbolist painter, who 'insisted with many determined gestures, that Symbolism said things which could not be said so perfectly in any other way, and needed but a right instinct for its understanding; while Allegory said things which could be said as well, or better, in another way, and needed a right knowledge for its understanding.' Although he admits that 'it is hard to say where Allegory and Symbolism melt into one another', I think his meaning is clear enough. The relationship between a symbol and the thing it symbolizes is natural and organic, whereas allegory makes an arbitrary equation between two things. A symbol, moreover, evokes a deeper response from the imagination because its outlines are flexible and undefined.

Kusta Ben Luka and his bride are too clearly Mr. and Mrs. Yeats in fancy dress, and no one else, while the Caliph—if my identification is correct—is a somewhat unsatisfactory representation of divinity. In his talk of game-bird and woman he may be every inch a Caliph, but he has none of the aura of supernatural power: he 'smells of mortality'. But if Yeats failed to find a fitting symbol in the sensuousness of Baghdad, he was to have more success in the remoter brilliance of Byzantium.

V

SAILING TO BYZANTIUM

I

1. That is no country for old men. The young
2. In one another's arms, birds in the trees
3. —Those dying generations—at their song,
4. The salmon-falls, the mackerel-crowded seas,
5. Fish, flesh, or fowl, commend all summer long
6. Whatever is begotten, born and dies.
7. Caught in that sensual music all neglect
8. Monuments of unageing intellect.

II

9. An aged man is but a paltry thing,
10. A tattered coat upon a stick, unless
11. Soul clap its hands and sing, and louder sing
12. For every tatter in its mortal dress,
13. Nor is there singing school but studying
14. Monuments of its own magnificence;
15. And therefore I have sailed the seas and come
16. To the holy city of Byzantium.

III

17. O sages standing in God's holy fire
18. As in the gold mosaic of a wall,
19. Come from the holy fire, perne in a gyre,
20. And be the singing-masters of my soul.
21. Consume my heart away; sick with desire
22. And fastened to a dying animal
23. It knows not what it is; and gather me
24. Into the artifice of eternity.

IV

25. Once out of nature I shall never take
26. My bodily form from any natural thing,
27. But such a form as Grecian goldsmiths make
28. Of hammered gold and gold enamelling
29. To keep a drowsy Emperor awake;
30. Or set upon a golden bough to sing
31. To lords and ladies of Byzantium
32. Of what is past, or passing, or to come.

So many critics have undertaken the journey to Yeats's Byzantium, explored it, mapped it, and marvelled at it, that one hesitates to follow lest one merely repeats their findings. Perhaps the most revealing journeys into the interior are those made by Jeffares[1] and Curtis Bradford[2] who, having had access to the manuscripts, are able to discuss the growth and history of 'Sailing to Byzantium' and 'Byzantium'.

Jeffares supports his argument with selected quotations from Yeats's typescripts, but clearly there is more to be learnt from a fuller investigation of the preliminary, and subsequent, manuscript drafts. These I had transcribed, and had reached my conclusions, before the publication of Curtis Bradford's article. Detailed and, in many ways, excellent as this is, it is not I think the last word on the Byzantine poems: one wonders, indeed, whether there can ever be a last word. Four manuscript folios which I believe to be relevant Curtis Bradford does not appear to have seen, and because I differ with many of his readings and certain of his findings I too presume to make the journey to Byzantium.

'Sailing to Byzantium' was written in the autumn of 1926. The

---

[1] 'The Byzantine Poems of W. B. Yeats', *Review of English Studies*, xxii, pp. 44–52.
[2] 'Yeats's Byzantium Poems', *P.M.L.A.*, lxxv, no. 1, pp. 110–25.

drafts are on sheets of two loose-leaf notebooks, which unfortunately Yeats did not number before they were removed: the ten
folios that are in pencil precede the two typescripts (which are
dated 26 September 1926), and the five in ink follow them. This
much is obvious from internal evidence, but the order in which
individual pencil or ink drafts were composed is less easy to deter-
mine, and my arrangement sometimes differs from Bradford's.
For the sake of simplicity I have numbered the sheets, manuscript
and typescript, from 1 to 19 in what seems to me their order of
composition.

Mrs. Yeats agrees with me that the poem probably began with
a tantalizingly illegible prose fragment of which Curtis Bradford
makes no mention:

F. 1r:

Now the day has come I will speak on of those

Loves have I had in play ⟨——————⟩

I will now

I will go now

Loves have had in play, (   )

That my soul loved (   )
                                    (   )
(   ) *that I loved in my first youth,*

    Now For many loves have I taken off my clothes
for some I threw them off in haste, for some slowly & indifferently

  & laid on my bed that I might ⟨———⟩ *be*
    ⟨———⟩ *they longed to see*
⟨——————⟩ *naked, but now I will take off my body*

*   *That they might be enfolded in that for which they*

*   *had longed*

  & (   ) *I live on love* (   )

      * Inserted from the bottom of the page.

(   ) *that which is my self alone*

(   )

(   )

O let me still be enfolded in my

& how shall we ever grow very

At first sight this appears to have no connexion at all with 'Sailing
to Byzantium'; although the paper on which and the pencil with
which it is written are identical with the other preliminary drafts.
Byzantium, its Emperor, sages, and golden bird are not mentioned
here; but the poet's scribbled meditation, for all its incoherence, is
following a familiar theme. Characteristically, his starting-point
is himself and the women that he has loved: characteristically again,
he starts with one who must surely be Maud Gonne:

That my soul loved (   )

(   ) that I loved in my first youth,

By contrast he passes to others that his body loved, rather than his
soul: 'Now For many loves have I taken off my clothes'. This, in
turn, leads to another contrast: '. . . but now I will take off my
body'. The opposition of soul and body, of course, foreshadows the
opposition of Byzantium and Ireland, although at this stage the
poet's mind is still preoccupied with the relationship of lover and
beloved. At the time of writing he was over sixty and conscious of
the presence of death. In November 1924 bad health and high
blood-pressure had driven him from Ireland to Italy and the
Mediterranean. As formerly he took off his clothes, he says, 'now I
will take off my body', so that the long-dead lovers of his youth may
'be enfolded in that for which they had longed'; namely his soul.

With thoughts of his former loves and future death uppermost
in his mind he begins on the first stanza. Bradford believes that:

The drafts of 'Sailing to Byzantium' begin with the protagonist's
voyage; the idea of first describing the country of the young, then
returning to the old age theme stated in line 1 and making old age the
reason for the journey occurred to Yeats during the process of composition.

I cannot think that Bradford would have come to this conclusion
if he had seen the three drafts of stanza I, and since there is no
evidence to suggest that Yeats wrote them at any time other than
at the beginning, I place them after the prose draft.

F. 2r: ~~Farewell friends from whom~~

So
     word
A good at, & last is farewell

This is no country for old men—if our Lord

~~Smiles~~

Is a smiling child upon his mother's knees

And in the hills ~~the old gods~~ those—I care not

What name I name them by—she here I love

(   )

~~All From all~~ the

From every song they sung (   )
                   for her sung

The most interesting thing about this fragment is that it contains
the germ of both the early and the late versions of stanza I. 'This
is no country for old men', however, does not appear again until
the stanza is remade after the first complete typescript. F. 3r shows
him still exploring the idea of the infant Christ:

F. 3r: Here all is young, & grows young day by day

Even my lord smiles (   )

Upon his mother's knees (   )

He struggles with this theme for a further eleven lines before
starting afresh on F. 4r:

All here—my god upon his mother's knees

Holds out his infant hands in play

~~*The old gods still at their*~~

~~*The gods*~~
   other
~~*Those older gods*~~

~~*All here—my god*~~

~~*Everything*~~
       my maker at his
All in this land—~~*even my god at*~~ *play*

Or else asleep upon his mother's knees
   ~~*And those*~~ *(————) as the mountain people say*
Those other gods that still—I have heard say

~~*Make love in shadow of the trees*~~

~~*Keep*~~ *are at their hunting & their gallantries*

Under the hills as in our thing day

The changing colour of the hill & seas
       very
All that men know think they know, ~~*is*~~ *young*

Cries that my tale is told my story sung

For the moment he points the opposition of youth and age by contrasting the infant Christ with the old gods of Irish mythology, but even the latter do not share the predicament of the ageing poet, since, though 'ancient' in the historic sense, they have the gift of perpetual youth. Yeats's stories in *The Celtic Twilight*, his early poetry and plays, all abound with references to Aengus, Master of Love, and such legendary figures as Baile and Aillinn, who live and love everlastingly among 'the gods of ancient Ireland the Tuatha De Danaan, or the Tribes of the Goddess Danu' in Tir-nan-Oge, the Country of the Young. A direct line of thought has brought Yeats from his initial prose meditation on those 'that I loved in my first youth', to:

   Those other gods that still—I have heard say

   ~~*Make love in shadow of the trees*~~

They, like the Caliph in 'The Gift of Harun Al-Rashid', who

divided his time between game-bird and woman, 'K̶e̶e̶p̶ are at their hunting & their gallantries.'

Here for the moment, it would seem, Yeats left stanza I, and on F. 5r passed to stanza II.

N̶o̶w̶ ̶I̶ ̶h̶a̶v̶e̶ ̶s̶h̶i̶p̶p̶e̶d̶ ̶a̶m̶o̶n̶g̶ ̶t̶h̶e̶s̶e̶ ̶m̶a̶r̶i̶n̶e̶r̶s̶

A̶n̶d̶ ̶s̶a̶i̶l̶ ̶s̶o̶u̶t̶h̶ ̶e̶a̶s̶t̶w̶a̶r̶d̶ ̶t̶o̶w̶a̶r̶d̶ ̶B̶y̶z̶a̶n̶t̶i̶u̶m̶

W̶h̶e̶r̶e̶ ̶i̶n̶ ̶t̶h̶e̶

B̶u̶t̶ ̶n̶o̶w̶ ̶I̶ ̶s̶a̶i̶l̶ ̶a̶m̶o̶n̶g̶ ̶t̶h̶e̶s̶e̶ ̶m̶a̶r̶i̶n̶e̶r̶s̶

F̶r̶o̶m̶ ̶t̶h̶i̶n̶g̶s̶ ̶b̶e̶c̶o̶m̶i̶n̶g̶ ̶t̶o̶ ̶t̶h̶e̶ ̶t̶h̶i̶n̶g̶ ̶b̶e̶c̶o̶m̶e̶

A̶n̶d̶ ̶s̶a̶i̶l̶ ̶s̶o̶u̶t̶h̶ ̶e̶a̶s̶t̶w̶a̶r̶d̶ ̶t̶o̶w̶a̶r̶d̶ ̶B̶y̶z̶a̶n̶t̶i̶u̶m̶

T̶h̶a̶t̶ ̶I̶ ̶m̶a̶y̶ ̶a̶n̶c̶h̶o̶r̶e̶d̶ ̶b̶y̶ ̶t̶h̶e̶ ̶m̶a̶r̶b̶l̶e̶ ̶s̶t̶a̶i̶r̶s̶

O̶ ̶w̶a̶t̶e̶r̶ ̶t̶h̶a̶t̶

A̶f̶t̶e̶r̶ ̶a̶ ̶d̶o̶z̶e̶n̶ ̶s̶t̶o̶r̶m̶s̶ ̶t̶o̶ ̶c̶o̶m̶e̶

I̶ ̶t̶h̶e̶r̶e̶f̶o̶r̶e̶ ̶v̶o̶y̶a̶g̶e̶ ̶t̶o̶w̶a̶r̶d̶s̶ ̶B̶y̶z̶a̶n̶t̶i̶u̶m̶

A̶m̶o̶n̶g̶ ̶t̶h̶e̶s̶e̶ ̶s̶u̶n̶ ̶b̶r̶o̶w̶n̶e̶d̶ ̶f̶r̶i̶e̶n̶d̶l̶y̶ ̶m̶a̶r̶i̶n̶e̶r̶s̶

A̶n̶o̶t̶h̶e̶r̶ ̶d̶o̶z̶e̶n̶ ̶d̶a̶y̶s̶ ̶&̶ ̶w̶e̶ ̶s̶h̶a̶l̶l̶ ̶c̶o̶m̶e̶

A̶m̶o̶n̶g̶ ̶t̶h̶e̶ ̶w̶a̶v̶e̶s̶ ̶t̶o̶ ̶w̶h̶e̶r̶e̶ ̶t̶h̶e̶ ̶n̶o̶i̶s̶e̶ ̶o̶f̶ ̶o̶a̶r̶s̶

U̶n̶d̶e̶r̶ ̶t̶h̶e̶ ̶s̶h̶a̶d̶o̶w̶ ̶o̶f̶ ̶i̶t̶s̶ ̶m̶a̶r̶b̶l̶e̶ ̶s̶t̶a̶i̶r̶s̶

Two of the three tentative openings to this stanza show clearly that something must have preceded it. 'But now I sail . . .' and 'I therefore voyage . . .' I regard as conclusive proof that stanza I was drafted first. The third opening he wisely thought best and carried it over to F. 6r:

N̶o̶w̶

I therefore travel towards Byzantium

Among these sun-browned pleasant mariners

Another dozen days & we shall come

Under the jetty & the marble stairs

Already I have learned by spout of foam
    Proves
~~*Creak of the sail's tackle, or of*~~ *the oars*

Can wake from the slumber where it lies

~~*The fish that*~~
        whereon souls ride to paradise
That fish the ~~*souls ride into paradise*~~

       nature to Byzantium
I fly ~~*from things becoming to the thing become*~~

~~*With creaking.*~~ *Among these sun browned pleasant mariners*

~~*(   ) To the gold & ivory*~~

~~*I seek for gold & ivory of Byzantium*~~

To begin with, the poet's imagination is dominated by the physical
approach to Byzantium, which he would have seen in 1924. The
symbolic level of interpretation has yet to be developed, and it is
something of a shock to pass from 'sail's tackle', and 'oars' to
'That fish the souls ride into paradise'. The imbalance is, however,
corrected when he begins the stanza again, with a new note of
urgency:

       nature to Byzantium
    I fly ~~*from things becoming to the thing become*~~

The 'gold & ivory', with which for two lines he experiments, have
also a suitable symbolic value because of their associations of rarity,
brilliance, purity, and great price. They were, of course, used
together by certain Greek sculptors.

       And gone are Phidias' famous ivories
       And all the golden grasshoppers and bees.

  With these at the forefront of his mind it would seem he started
on F. 7r:

    Or Phidias

      Flying from nature
    ~~*Therefore I travel*~~ *towards Byzantium*

Among these dark skinned pleasant mariners

I long for St. Sophia's sacred dome
              ~~on pale, columned~~
~~That I may look column~~   ~~dome~~

~~A statue by Phidias~~   stairs

~~Statues of Phidias~~

Mirrored in water where a glint of foam
              ~~the splashing~~
~~Proves that noise   , or~~

~~But demonstrates that splash or creak of oar~~
    ~~But proves~~ But demonstrates the
~~Proves~~ that ~~the sudden splashing of the oar~~
      startle   ~~creaking or~~ the splash of oars,
Can ~~wake~~ from the slumber where it lies

That fish that bears the soul to paradise

~~That I may look on the great churches dome~~

~~Statues of bronze over a marble stair~~
      walls of gold & ivory
~~For (_____) marble stairs~~

Mirror like water where a glint of foam

But demonstrates the sudden falling oars

This sheet has been cancelled with a diagonal line. Still Yeats is preoccupied with the physical aspect of Byzantium, and introduces the great dome of Hagia Sophia. On F. 8r a new element enters stanza II:

~~This Danish merchant on a relic swears~~

~~That he will~~ be

~~All that afflicts me, but this merchant swears~~

~~To bear me eastward to Byzantium~~

But now these pleasant dark skinned mariners

> ~~Carry Bear~~
> *Carry me toward that great Byzantium*
>   *And ageless beauty where age is living*
> ~~Where nothing changes~~ *singing to the oars*
>   *on the great shining*
> *That I may look ~~on St Sophia's~~ Dome*
>   *or upon*
> ~~On Phidias' marble, or a marble stairs,~~
>
> *On mirroring waters where a glint*
>
> ~~On mirroring waters, upon sudden foam~~
>
> *   *On gold limbed saints & emperors*
>
> *   *After the mirroring waters & the foam*
>
> *Where the dark drowsy fins a moment rise*
>   *carry*
> *Of fish, that ~~bear~~ souls to Paradise.*

The first question to be asked here is who is the merchant? Mrs.
Yeats recalls that her husband had long talks with a Danish merchant when they were travelling by sea, not, as one might expect,
to the Mediterranean in 1924, but earlier in that year to Stockholm
for the Nobel celebrations. This is a possible explanation of the
reference, but not of why Yeats chose to include it in his poem.
Bradford quotes an interesting and relevant note from a manuscript
book begun at Oxford, 7 April 1921: 'I had just finished a poem in
which a poet of the Middle Ages besought the saints "in the holy
fire" to send their ecstasy.' He therefore concludes that 'in the
early drafts Yeats is consciously medievalizing; the "poet of the
Middle Ages" gradually disappears until the action of the finished
poem is timeless, recurrent, eternal.' His view is confirmed by a
passage which Yeats wrote to accompany a reading from his poems
over B.B.C. Belfast on 8 September 1931. He omitted both text
and comment from the final script:

Now I am trying to write about the state of my soul, for it is right
for an old man to make his soul, and some of my thoughts upon that
subject I have put into a poem called 'Sailing to Byzantium'. When
Irishmen were illuminating the Book of Kells and making the jewelled

---

* Inserted from the foot of the page.

croziers in the National Museum, Byzantium was the centre of European civilization and the source of its spiritual philosophy, so I symbolize the search for the spiritual life by a journey to that city.

The Book of Kells was illuminated in the eighth century, the Danes occupied Dublin from the ninth to the twelfth centuries, and Yeats is describing Byzantium as it was 'towards the end of the first Christian millenium'.[1]

F. 8r shows a further advance on F. 7r, because in stressing the 'ageless beauty' of Byzantium, 'where nothing changes', Yeats expands his symbol of the life of the intellect and the life hereafter. Again, there is here the first mention of 'gold limbed saints and emperors', who were finally to become 'sages standing in God's holy fire'. The poet is alluding, on a literal plane, to figures in a mosaic, but there has been some doubt as to what mosaic he had in mind, if indeed he was thinking of a particular mosaic at all.[2] Hone records that Yeats went to Sicily in November 1924, 'the attraction there being . . . the Byzantine mosaics of Monreale and the Capella Palatina at Palermo'.[3] At Céphalu he would have seen a splendid mosaic of Christ Pantocrator, but Mrs. Yeats tells me that they visited the cathedral on a dark day, and he was much more excited during their visit to Monreale. Lines on F. 6v, however, prove that in this instance Yeats drew his inspiration from Ravenna, which he had visited in 1907:

> aged
> And most of all an old thought harried me
>
> Standing in gold on church or pedestal
>
> Angel, vestal or emperors lost in gold[4]
> wave of
> O dolphin haunted, & flooding gold
> might
> fold
> sight
> bold

There is in the church of San Apollinare Nuovo a frieze consisting

---

[1] Yeats's 1930 diary: see p. 115.
[2] Bradford speaks of Yeats's 'imagined mosaic'.
[3] W. B. Yeats, 1865–1939, 1942, p. 367.
[4] Bradford reads: Angel visible or emperors . . .

of two great panels. Against a common background of gold stand, in the one, the holy virgins, and in the other, the holy martyrs. These noble figures must have been in Yeats's mind when he wrote 'Angel, vestal or emperors lost in gold': on F. 8v they become 'Saints & apostles'.

> Procession on procession, tier on tier
>
> Saints & apostles in the gold of a wall
>
> ~~As though it were God's love await~~
>
> ~~Symbolic of God's love await my prayer~~
>
> ~~Turn their old withered heads & wait my prayer~~
>
> ~~Or into sea like~~   tier
>
> ~~Or lost~~   wall
>
> ~~As if God's love~~   were
>
> ~~As if God's burning heart awaits my prayer~~
>
> ~~To fill me with~~
>
> As in God's love will refuse my prayer
>
> When prostrate on the marble step I fall
>
> ~~And cry amid my tears~~
>
> And cry aloud—'I sicken with desire
>   And
> ~~Though~~ fastened to a dying animal
>
> Cannot endure my life—O gather me
>
> Into the artifice of eternity!

In the poet's violent statement of his personal predicament (the latter part of which seems to have occurred to him spontaneously) we see physical details being absorbed into the symbolic meaning. 'The gold of a wall' and the 'marble step' are no longer simply local colour introduced for a pictorial effect, but rather a deliberate opposition of heat and cold, future life and present death. Though

the reference to God, like that in the first drafts of stanza I, was
later abandoned—except in the phrase 'God's holy fire'—it acts
as a signpost to the emperor of stanza IV.

This is already half formed at its first appearance on F. 9*r*:

> *& if it be the Dolphin's back*   take
>   spring
>   sake
>
> *Of hammered gold & gold enamelling*
>
> *That the Greek goldsmiths make*
>
> *And set in golden leaves to sing*
>
> *Of present past & future & to come*
>
> *For the instruction of Byzantium*

There is here an obvious echo of Blake:

> Here the voice of the Bard!
> Who present, past and future sees;

Perhaps for that reason Yeats altered his lines when he continued
the stanza on F. 10*r*:

> ~~And if I stride the~~
>   *the sensual stream being past I shall not*[1]
> ~~If it must be the Dolphin I shall~~ *take*
>
> *No shifting form of nature's fashioning*
>   *But such a form as Grecian*
> ~~The stream being past but such as~~ *goldsmiths make*[2]

After these cramped and crossed-out lines, the poet's writing which
is so often an index of his inspiration, quickens, and runs boldly
to the stanza's triumphant end.

> *Of hammered gold & gold enamelling*
>
> *At the emperor's order for his Lady's sake*
>
> *And set upon a golden bough to sing*
>
> *To lords & ladies of Byzantium*
>
> *Of what is past, or passing or to come*

[1] Bradford reads: The sensual shears . . .   [2] Bradford reads: The shears being . . .

At this point, still on F. 10r, he goes back to stanza III:

> *O saints that stand amid God's sacred fire*
>
> *As in the gold mosaic of a wall*
> * Consume this heart   it*
> *~~Transfigure me~~ & make ~~me~~ what you were*
> * Unwavering, indifferent, fanatical*
> *~~Rigid, abstracted, & fantastical~~ ~~fanatical~~*
> * It faints upon the road*
> *~~The body burned away~~—sick with desire*
> * But*
> *~~Being~~ fastened to this dying animal*
>
> *O send the dolphins back & gather me*
>
> *Into the artifice of eternity.*

The dolphin, upon whose back the dead ride from time to eternity, Yeats has carried over from F. 9r to F. 10r. When he abandons it, he yet retains the idea of a symbolic sea voyage in the phrase 'The sensual stream'. This reading is supported by Yeats's description of his poem in a passage cancelled from the manuscript of his unpublished lecture 'Modern Ireland'. 'I have pictured the ghosts swimming, mounted upon dolphins, through the sensual seas.'[1] Bradford's reading, 'The sensual shears' (of Atropos, understood) is almost certainly wrong.

Much has been written of the golden bird. Dume[2] has convincingly traced the reference to passages in Gibbon's *Decline and Fall* and *The Cambridge Mediaeval History*, both of which Yeats had bought with his Nobel prize money in 1923. Gibbon says that the Emperor of Byzantium caused his golden tree to be made in emulation of the Caliph of Baghdad, which further supports my contention that Yeats came to the former by way of Harun Al-Rashid. Stauffer, on no evidence at all, calls the bird a nightingale; Macneice[3] calls it a metal cock. An equally good case might be made out for a 'burnished dove'[4] since Aeneas was guided to his

---

[1] Quoted by Bradford.

[2] 'Yeats's Golden Tree and Birds in the Byzantine Poems', *Modern Language Notes*, lxvii, pp. 404–7.

[3] *The Poetry of W. B. Yeats*, 1941, p. 141.

[4] 'The Indian to His Love', *Variorum*, p. 77.

golden bough, which could alone gain him admittance to the
Underworld, by his mother's doves:

> inde ubi venere ad fauces grave olentis Averni,
> tollunt se celeres liquidumque per aera lapsae
> sedibus optatis gemina super arbore sidunt,
> discolor unde auri per ramos aura refulsit.[1]

Yeats in this poem, however, does not specify the nature of his
golden bird, and we should resist the temptation to do so for him.
It is enough that we remember that he frequently depicts the souls
of the dead as birds. In *The Shadowy Waters*, for instance, Forgael
says:

> When men die
> They are changed and as grey birds fly out to sea.

and in *Deidre* the first musician makes his ominous prophecy of
the lovers' union in death: 'Eagles have gone into their cloudy bed.'
Yeats chooses a bird as symbol of his own disembodied soul, because in that form he can continue his singing in Byzantium; and
he chooses gold because it suggests brightness, richness, permanence, refinement, and incorruptibility.

The Emperor and his Lady may well have originated as Justinian
and Theodora. In *A Vision* Yeats speaks of 'the Emperor himself
who is a God dependant upon a greater God',[2] and, as several
critics have noted, the Emperor in the two Byzantium poems is
clearly a symbol of divinity. The 'lords & ladies of Byzantium' can
only be the spirits of the noble dead:

> the lords and ladies gay
> That were beaten into clay
> Through seven heroic centuries.

In the draft of stanza III on F. 10r every line but the last has been
altered. The 'gold of a wall' has become the sacred fire of purifica-
tion, and the poet no longer addresses himself directly to the deity,
but to the saints that are already in the fire. They are, as it were,
the 'doorkeepers in the house of the Lord'. The stanza has been
tightened considerably, but is still further from its finished shape
than stanza IV.

[1] Virgil, *Aeneid*, Book VI, lines 201–4.   [2] 1925 edition, p. 189.

It would seem that having reached this stage in the composition of his poem, Yeats called for the typewriter. The first full draft is in typescript, with stanzas I and II on one sheet, III and IV on another. Of this draft there are two copies: both sheets 1 and one sheet 2 show inked corrections in Yeats's hand, so I transcribe the first sheet with the latest revisions and the revised second sheet. Unlike Bradford, whose transcription—though clear—is misleading,[1] I do not separate the typescript from its inked revisions; but simply print the former in roman and the hand-writing in italic:

F. 13*r*:   TOWARDS BYZANTIUM

> *Here all is young ; the chapel walls display*
> All in this land—my Maker that is play
> *My God* An infant sleeping on
> Or else asleep upon His Mother's knees
> *   *Weary with toil Teig sleeps till break of day*
> *Teig (   ) his days (   ) at break of day*
> Others, that as the mountain people say
> *(   ) That other drowsy with night's gallantries*[2]
> Are at their hunting and their gallantries
> *Has snored the* drowsy morning *morning's dreary light away*[2]
> Under the hills as in our fathers' day
> *   *toiled & loved*
> *   *I have* slept *slept my nights away like these*[2]
> *Being young I toiled (   ) the night's & the day's sleep like*
>   *these*
>
> The changing colours of the hills and seas
>   *Lost in a glistening labyrinth that a snail   of leaves*
>
> *A* | All that men know or think they know, being young
> *scrawls*| *(——————) mirror of the soul*
> *upon* | Cry that my tale is told my story sung

This draft clarifies certain points. The change from 'Here', in line 1 of the manuscript version, to 'this land', sharpens the con-trast between Ireland and Byzantium. In both typescript versions

---

[1] He makes it appear as if Yeats completely over-wrote his typescript, which is not the case.

[2] Bradford reads Yeats's corrections as:

> *That other wearied with night's gallantries*
> *Sleeps the morning and the noon away*
> *I have toiled and loved until I slept like these*

These lines, however, are to be found on the earlier typescript, F. 11*r*.

* Line inserted from the top of the page.

of this line there is an obvious misprint. Yeats, I suspect, dictating
over his typist's shoulder, said: 'All in this land—my Maker at his
play' which was mis-heard as: 'All in this land—my Maker that
is play'. The Madonna and child are shown to be depicted on the
chapel walls, and so anticipate the later 'Saints & apostles in the
gold of a wall'. In his corrections Yeats has introduced Teig(ue),
the visionary fool found also in *The Hourglass*, who typifying the
Irish peasant, is balanced against the Irish aristocrat, '. . . that
other drowsy with night's gallantries'. The poet, who liked to
think of himself as representing peasantry and aristocracy alike,
resolves the antithesis in synthesis: 'I have toiled & loved my
nights away like these'. At this stage the only reference to the
poet's song, which was to become a dominant theme, is that in the
last line, which he cuts out in his corrections. F. 13*r* continues
with stanza II:

> *But now I   to*
> ~~I therefore~~ travel ~~towards~~ Byzantium
> *With many a dark skinned*
> ~~Among these sun-brown~~ pleasant mariners
>   *I*
> Another dozen days and ~~we~~ shall come
>
> Under the jetty and the marble stair

Under these lines the stanza is re-formed:

> *With many a*
> ~~But now these~~ pleasant dark skinned mariners
> *Carries*
> ~~Carry~~ me towards that great Byzantium
>
> Where all is ancient, singing at the oars
>
> That I may look in the great churches dome
>
> On gold-embedded saints and emperors
>
> After the mirroring waters and the foam
>
> Where the great drowsy fins a moment rise
>
> Of fish that carry souls to Paradise.

Still dissatisfied, Yeats has crossed out these lines. They show no

great advance on the manuscript drafts, but at the foot of the page
he has scribbled:

> *And after to unwinking wisdom's home*
>
> *The marvel of the world & gardens where*
>
> ~~*This ageing body shall be no defect*~~
>
> ~~*(   ) in this change of country intellect*~~
>
> ~~*This ageing body shall be no defect*~~

This theme he has pursued along the left-hand edge of the page:

> *Transfigurations of the intellect*
>
> *Can cure this ageing body of defect*

and again:

> ~~*Men choose companions for their*~~
>
> ~~*In the discourse of joyous*~~ *intellect*
>
> ~~*This ageing body shall be no defect*~~

In these confused fragments we see a new second stanza taking
shape. Yeats no longer looks outwards in the direction of Byzantium, but inwards to the struggle of his intellect (or soul) to break
free from 'this ageing body'. The 'unwinking wisdom' was probably suggested by a mosaic face, perhaps that of the Céphalu Christ
Pantocrator.

On F. 14r begins the typescript stanza III:

> *Transfigured saints that move amid the*
> ~~O saints thats stand amid God's sacred fire~~
>
> As in the gold mosaic of a wall
> *Transform*
> ~~Consume~~ this heart and make it what you were
>
> ~~It faints upon the road sick with desire~~
> *Unfaltering|* ~~Unwavering,~~ indifferent, fanatical
> ~~But fastened to this dying animal~~
>
> It faints upon the road sick with desire
>
> But fastened to this dying animal

> Or send the dolphins back, and gather me
>
> Into the artifice of eternity

This shows no advance on the manuscript draft, but following it is an altered stanza IV:

> The sensuous dream being past I shall not take
>   guttering
> A ~~shifting~~ form of nature's fashioning
>
> But rather that the Grecian smithies make
>
> Of hammered gold and gold enamelling
>
> At the Emperor's order for his lady's sake
>
> And set upon a golden bough to sing
>
> To lords and ladies of Byzantium
>
> Of what is past or passing or to come.

Sept 26 1926

'Sensual stream' has been altered to 'sensuous dream'; 'shifting' to the more powerful 'guttering'; 'such' has been momentarily dropped from line 27, and 'the Grecian goldsmiths' changed to 'the Grecian smithies'.

At this point, contrary to his general practice, Yeats returned to rough manuscript drafts on loose-leaf sheets: on F. 15r he starts the poem again, abandoning his original opening stanza, and striking out in a new direction:

> ~~Here~~
>   *That*
> ~~This~~ *is no country for old men—the young*
>   *That travel singing*
> ~~Pass by me sing~~ *of their loves, the trees*
>   *Clad*
> ~~Break~~ *in such foliage that it seems a song*
>
> *The shadow of the birds upon the seas*
>
> ~~The herring in the seas,~~
>
> ~~The fish in shoals,~~

~~The leaping fish, the fields all summer long~~

~~Praise ( ) with a ( ) great monument~~

~~Praise Plenty's horn, but no great monument~~
    The crowding fish
~~The leaping fish~~ commend all summer long
      Plenty,
( ) ~~abundance~~ but no monument[1]

Commends the never ageing intellect
        mackerel
The salmon rivers, the ~~fish~~ crowded seas
~~All flesh~~   spring all
~~Flesh,~~ Fish, flesh & fowl, all summer long

~~What Commemorate what is begot & dies.~~

But praise what is begotten, born & dies

~~And no man raises up a monument~~

~~To the unbegotten intellect~~

~~And man has made no mighty monument~~

~~To praise the unbegotten intellect~~

This page was cancelled with a diagonal line. There is now no
reference to the infant Christ or the Gods of Irish mythology.
Teig, and more importantly, the 'I' figure, have been also withdrawn to make way for the more symbolic 'Fish, flesh & fowl'.
The poem's horizons are constantly expanding, and the peculiarly
Irish nature of the landscape fades into the universal. Henn and
others have properly pointed out that salmon and mackerel would
have Irish associations for Yeats, but they are not, of course,
found only in Irish waters. Confronted now with the abundant
energy of the natural world, he sees that 'all flesh is grass' and that
only the unregarded intellect is never ageing. On F. 16r his ideas
are ordered and compressed within the tight frame of the stanza:

              ~~the trees~~

      ~~Those dying generations at their song~~

[1] Bradford reads: Deceiving (?) ~~abundance~~ . . .

The salmon leap, the mackerel crowded seas

That is no country for old men; the young

In one another's arms, birds in the trees

Those dying generations at their song,

The salmon falls, the mackerel crowded seas

Fish flesh & fowl, all spring & summer long

Extoll what is begotten, born & dies

And man has made no monument to extoll

The unbegotten wisdom of the soul

The unborn, undying, unbegotten soul

The 'all-flesh-is-grass' theme is here brought into greater prominence with the beautiful, elegiac phrase, 'Those dying generations'.
'The young in one another's arms', and 'birds in the trees' are
balanced against each other with just enough artifice to suggest that
neither young nor birds will maintain their position indefinitely.
These natural birds, of course, anticipate the artificial golden bird
that time cannot dislodge from its golden bough; just as the salmon
and mackerel anticipate the symbolic dolphins of 'Byzantium'.
'Spring and summer' imply the approaching presence of winter
and the 'killing frost'. In substance the stanza's end is unchanged,
but Yeats is still groping for words to express his meaning. Where
previously he had said, 'man has made no mighty monument To
praise the unbegotten intellect', he now speaks of 'no monument
to extoll The unborn, undying, unbegotten soul'.

   Stanza II is transformed no less radically than stanza I in this
great secondary blaze of inspiration: on F. 17r he gropes after the
elusive shape of a new idea:

> *What has being old*
>   *An*
> *The aged man is but a paltry thing*
>
> *An old man is a paltry*

~~A paltry business to be old,~~ unless
               its hands   louder sing
~~My~~ Soul clap its ~~hands~~ & sing, & ~~then sing more~~

                                  dress

                                 oar

~~For~~

~~For every tatter~~

~~For every morsel torn out of the dress~~[1]

~~As time wears out~~

~~It is a paltry business to be old~~

For every tatter in its mortal dress

Critics detect here a recollection of Blake's vision in which he saw the soul of his dead brother carried up to heaven, clapping its hands for joy. Yeats is haunted by the word 'paltry', but cannot place it to his satisfaction until he comes to F. 15v:

An aged man is but a paltry thing

Nature has cast him like a shoe unless

Soul clap its hands & sing, & louder sing

For every tatter in its mortal dress
       And there's no singing school like studying[2]
~~And come upon that mood is studying~~
                own
The monuments of its ~~old~~ magnificence

~~And for that reason~~ have

And therefore have I sailed the seas & come

To the holy city of Byzantium

Gone now from stanza II are the mariners, the jetty, the marble stair, and the fish: dome, saints, and emperor are reserved for the

---

[1] Bradford reads: For every mortal born out of the dress
[2] Inserted from the foot of the page.

later stanzas. As in the revision of stanza I, husk has been stripped away and the kernel laid bare. The central theme is stated objectively, and, with the first hint of the scarecrow image ('cast . . . shoe', 'tatter in its mortal dress', later to be 'tattered coat upon a stick'), acts as a prologue preparing for the poet's own dramatic entrance:

> *And therefore have I sailed the seas & come*
>
> *To the holy city of Byzantium.*

Reducing his original stanza to this couplet, Yeats has retained only one epithet to describe the city. Ellman says correctly that: 'Byzantium is a holy city, because it is the capital of Eastern Christendom, but it is also Yeats's holy city of the imagination, as Golgonooza was Blake's',[1] but he ignores what is surely a primary meaning. Byzantium is holy—the word is repeated twice: 'God's holy fire', and 'the holy fire'—because in the life after death one is in the presence of God. Yeats tells us in *A Vision* that at the middle of the fifth century, 'Byzantium became Byzantine and substituted for formal Roman magnificence, with its glorification of physical power, an architecture that suggests the Sacred City in the Apocalypse of St. John'.[2] The 'Roman magnificence with its glorification of physical power' may well have been at the back of his mind when he contrasted 'Monuments of unageing intellect' with 'Monuments of its own magnificence'. The 'its' presumably refers to every 'singing school' that has abandoned its true creative function for this self-regarding study.

Stanza III at this stage did not need the drastic remodelling of the two that preceded it, but F. 18r shows Yeats still far from satisfied:

> *O saints amid the gold mosaic of a*
>   *& martyrs in God's*
> *O saints* ~~amid the gold~~ *amid God's holy fire*
>
> *As in the gold mosaic of a wall*
>
> ~~Look down upon me sickened with desire~~

---

[1] *Yeats/The Man and the Masks*, 1949, p. 257.
[2] 1925 edition, p. 190.

> ~~And fastened to this dying animal~~
>   Immovable
> ~~Immovable,~~ or moving in a gyre

This he crossed out, and started again below:

> O sages standing in God's holy fire
>
> As in the gold mosaic of a wall
>   perning
> Come from the holy fire, ~~perne~~ in a gyre
>
> And be the singing masters of my soul
>
> That knows not what it is, sick with desire
>
> And fastened to a dying animal
>
> Or send the dolphins back and gather me
>
> Into the artifice of eternity

The 'saints' have become 'sages', and, for the first time, are asked to 'be the singing masters of my soul', thereby remedying the lack of 'singing-school'. The dolphins, who here enter the poem unannounced and unexplained, make their last appearance in 'Sailing to Byzantium' in the first line of stanza IV on F. 19*r*:

> The Dolphin's journey done I shall not take
>
> ~~Form~~ My bodily form from any natural thing
>
> But such a form as Grecian goldsmiths make
>
> Of hammered gold & gold enamelling
>
> At the emperor's order for his lady's sake
>
> And set upon a golden bough to sing
>
> To lords ladies of Byzantium
>
> Of what is past or present or to come.

'A guttering form' is here replaced by 'My bodily form', 'smithies' by 'goldsmiths', and 'passing' (in the last line) to 'present'. Happily, the first reading was subsequently restored.

The finished version of the poem shows yet another stage of development to have taken place. Lines 5–8 were altered to read:

> Fish, flesh, or fowl, commend all summer long
> Whatever is begotten, born, and dies,
> Caught in that sensual music all neglect
> Monuments of unageing intellect.

The tripartite subject of the first sentence, 'Fish, flesh, or fowl,' is delicately balanced against a tripartite object, 'Whatever is begotten, born, and dies'. 'The sensual stream' mentioned in an early draft of stanza IV has become a 'sensual music': and the song of the natural 'fowl' prepares for the antiphonal, intellectual music of the bird on the golden bough.

In revising stanza II, Yeats defined the scarecrow image more clearly; altering 'Nature has cast him like a shoe unless . . .' to 'A tattered coat upon a stick, unless . . .'. Between the fourth and the fifth printings he made two further changes. 'And there's no singing school . . .' became 'Nor is there singing school . . .'. The new reading is more dignified, and slows down the colloquial pace of the stanza's opening in preparation for its resounding close. The second alteration, 'have I' to 'I have', removes an over-literary inversion and again slows the movement of the line.

In the finished stanza III, the 'sages' are requested to do three things. Firstly, to:

> Come from the holy fire, perne in a gyre,
> And be the singing-masters of my soul.

The close internal rhyme of 'fire' and 'gyre' brilliantly suggests a narrowing spiral and the approaching climax. Secondly, they are asked to:

> Consume my heart away; sick with desire
> And fastened to a dying animal

The change from the demonstrative 'this' to the indefinite 'a dying animal', was incorporated at the third printing, and is a marked improvement in that it implies an even greater detachment between the soul and its clogging body. Once the 'sages' have fulfilled his first two requests, they are asked to 'gather me Into the artifice of eternity.' Here as at the start of the final stanza, the dolphins are seen no longer. They returned to grow large in the sea of Yeats's conscious and subconscious mind, before rising so magnificently to the surface in 'Byzantium'.

Stanza IV now opens with the more significant antithesis of 'out of nature' and 'any natural thing'. Finally, the Emperor's 'lady' follows the Virgin Mary (of stanza I) and the 'vestals' (of stanza III) out of the poem. Her departure properly concentrates the reader's attention on the 'drowsy emperor', and it is interesting to see the epithet 'drowsy' salvaged from two abandoned lines: 'That other drowsy with night's gallantries', and 'Where the great drowsy fins a moment rise'. As Bradford points out, this omission avoids the awkward repetition of 'lady's' with 'ladies' in line 31. I am not altogether convinced by his further suggestion that the 'chivalric idea' of the 'emperor's lady' was 'a final touch of medievalizing that had to go lest it interfere with the timelessness of the finished poem'. I think it more likely that Yeats, anxious to keep his symbols timeless, removed a lady who might be identified as the Empress Theodora at the side of Justinian, or even the Virgin Mary beside the Christian God. That Yeats's symbol of the deity should be in danger of falling asleep, but for the singing of Yeats's soul, is a revealing commentary on the poet's view of God and of himself.

I shall examine in the next chapter how he made his journey to within sight of Byzantium, and returned to develop these themes still further.

VI

BYZANTIUM

1. The unpurged images of day recede;
2. The Emperor's drunken soldiery are abed;
3. Night resonance recedes, night-walkers' song
4. After great cathedral gong;
5. A starlit or a moonlit dome disdains
6. All that man is,
7. All mere complexities,
8. The fury and the mire of human veins.

9. Before me floats an image, man or shade,
10. Shade more than man, more image than a shade;
11. For Hades' bobbin bound in mummy-cloth
12. May unwind the winding path;
13. A mouth that has no moisture and no breath
14. Breathless mouths may summon;
15. I hail the superhuman;
16. I call it death-in-life and life-in-death.

17. Miracle, bird or golden handiwork,
18. More miracle than bird or handiwork,
19. Planted on the star-lit golden bough,
20. Can like the cocks of Hades crow,
21. Or, by the moon embittered, scorn aloud
22. In glory of changeless metal
23. Common bird or petal
24. And all complexities of mire or blood.

25. At midnight on the Emperor's pavement flit
26. Flames that no faggot feeds, nor steel has lit,

27. Nor storm disturbs, flames begotten of flame,
28. Where blood-begotten spirits come
29. And all complexities of fury leave,
30. Dying into a dance,
31. An agony of trance,
32. An agony of flame that cannot singe a sleeve.

33. Astraddle on the dolphin's mire and blood,
34. Spirit after spirit! The smithies break the flood,
35. The golden smithies of the Emperor!
36. Marbles of the dancing floor
37. Break bitter furies of complexity,
38. Those images that yet
39. Fresh images beget,
40. That dolphin-torn, that gong-tormented sea.

IN a note to his *Collected Poems* Yeats says that he wrote 'Byzantium' to 'warm himself back into life'. He had been perilously near death from Malta fever at Rapallo during the autumn of 1929, and the following spring there appeared in his diary the first shoot of the quickening poem. The entry is dated 30 April (1930), and reads:

Subject for a poem
Describe Byzantium as it is in the system towards the end of the first

Christian millenium. ~~The worn ascetics on the walls contrasted with their (?)~~

~~splendour. A walking mummy. A spiritual refinement and perfection amid~~

~~a rigid world. A sigh of wind—autumn leaves in the streets. The divine born~~

~~amidst natural decay.~~

In ink of a different colour, therefore probably later, Yeats wrote over the cancelled lines:

A walking mummy; flames at the street corners where the soul is purified.

Birds of hammered gold singing in the golden trees. In the harbour (dolphins)

offering their backs to the wailing dead that they may carry them to para-

dise. These subjects have been in my head for some time, especially the last.

How long these subjects had been in his head we know from the previous chapter: his symbols were almost fully developed before he began the second poem.

On 16 April 1930 Sturge Moore wrote to Yeats:

Your 'Sailing to Byzantium', magnificent as the first three stanzas are, lets me down in the fourth, as such a goldsmith's bird is as much nature as a man's body, especially if it only sings like Homer and Shakespeare of what is past or passing or to come to Lords and Ladies.[1]

Yeats, it would seem, took this criticism to heart, and a fortnight

[1] Ursula Bridge, *W. B. Yeats and T. Sturge Moore*, 1953, p. 162.

later wrote his prose 'Subject for a poem'. By the middle of June he had done a complete version of the poem, and on 4 October wrote to Sturge Moore:

The poem originates from a criticism of yours. You objected to the last verse of 'Sailing to Byzantium' because a bird made by a goldsmith was just as natural as anything else. That showed me that the idea needed exposition.[1]

The growth of 'Byzantium' is traced more easily than that of 'Sailing to Byzantium', since the manuscript appears on thirteen pages of Manuscript Book B. With one exception the pages are consecutive, and I have numbered them for my purposes, 1–14, although this is far from being the first poem in the book. Yeats generally began on the right-hand page of the opening and later did his corrections on the left. His first draft therefore is on page 2, which is headed by his rhyme scheme: AABBCDDCC: this he had already used to good effect in 'In Memory of Major Robert Gregory' and 'A Prayer for my Daughter'. Page 2 is written in ink:

When (———) *all*

~~*When all that roaring rout of rascals*~~ (———) *are a bed*

~~*When every roaring rascal is a bed*~~

~~*When the last brawler's tumbled into bed,*~~

~~*When the emperor's brawling soldiers are bed*~~

~~*When the last brawler tumbles into bed*~~

a
When the emperor's brawling soldiers are bed,

~~*When the last*~~

~~*When the last*~~

~~*The last robber*~~

~~*The last benighted robber or army fled*~~

[1] Ursula Bridge, *W. B. Yeats and T. Sturge Moore*, 1953, p. 164.

~~When the last~~

~~The last robber or his~~
    thieves' last benighted traveller
The ~~night thieves' latest victim~~ *dead or fled,*

~~Silence fallen~~
    When
~~When starlit purple~~
             ~~beats down~~
~~When death like sleep has destroys the harlot's song~~

~~And the great cathedral gong~~

~~When~~

And silence falls on the cathedral gong

And the drunken harlot's song

Even as he struggles with his opening lines he has the symbolic nature of Byzantium fixed clearly in his mind. 'When death like sleep has destroys the harlot's curse' is an obvious echo of Blake's poem about another symbolic city—'London'—where

        the hapless soldier's sigh
Runs in blood down palace walls.

But most through midnight streets I hear
How the youthful harlot's curse
Blasts the new-born infant's tear.

The resemblances are too strong for coincidence: soldier, palace (suggesting emperor?), 'midnight streets', and the 'harlot's curse'.

On page 1 Yeats gathers his scattered threads together into a single stanza:

I

When the emperor's brawling soldiers are a bed

The last benighted victim dead or fled;
    When
~~And~~ *silence falls on the cathedral gong*

And the drunken harlot's song

> *a*
> ~~On~~ *cloudy silence, or a silence lit*
>
> *Whether by star or moon*
>
> *I tread the emperor's town,*
>
> *All my intricacies grown clear & sweet*

The fact of compression appears in the succession of antitheses: soldiers/victim, cathedral gong/harlot's song, cloudy silence/silence lit, star/moon. An impression of the whole, complicated, physical world that is his port of departure for a spiritual world, he has packed into six lines. 'The emperor's brawling soldiers', together with victim and harlot, represent mankind (the children of God). After their 'sound and fury' the striking contrast of silence and star or moon marks the poet's transition to another sphere.

> *I tread the emperor's town,*
>
> *All my intricacies grown clear & sweet*

The verse movement is immediately more tranquil, and the companion vowels of 'clear' and 'sweet' give an effect of cool purity and welcome relief after the fevered squalour of the first four lines. Bradford points out that 'intricacies' is a keyword of the first draft, and is replaced in the second draft by 'complexities'. As in the first drafts of 'Sailing to Byzantium' Yeats makes no attempt to withhold his own entrance (or that of the 'I' protagonist) into the poem, but says 'I tread the emperor's town'.

Lower on page 1 he begins again, in pencil:

> *All the tumultuous floods of day recede*
>
> *Soldiers, robbers, victims are in their beds*
>
> *Night's resonance recedes—night walker's song*
>
> *After cathedral gong;*
>
> ~~*I tread among the dark intricacies*~~
>
> ~~*But a*~~
>
> *I traverse all the town's intricacies*

~~A starry glittering~~

~~All the town becomes~~

Under the starlight dome;

And things there become,

~~Blood begotten shades & images~~

~~A mystery of shades & images~~

~~Mummies or blood begotten images~~
   and   & hallowed
Mummies, ~~or~~ shades ~~or stony~~ images

Here, with the second stanza beginning to grow out of the first, we see the poet probing deeper symbolic levels. 'The tumultuous floods of day' anticipate the great image of the final stanza: the harlots have faded into 'night-walkers', and seem almost as much a part of the night itself as their song is part of the 'night resonance'. The 'starlight dome' of St. Sophia, which he calls elsewhere 'an image for the Holy Wisdom', opposes 'dark intricacies' with its calm, bright symmetry.

In the closing lines of page 1 he had been confronted by 'Mummies, or shades or stony images', but by the time Yeats started on page 3 he would seem to have conceived the idea of a single guide, who would lead him through Byzantium as the Sibyl led Aeneas, and Virgil led Dante. This, presumably, is the 'walking mummy' of the prose draft.

      cloth

      path

      light as a breath

~~His breathless snores & seems to beckon me~~
        beckons
His breathless body ~~moves & summons~~ me;
 name it
~~I call that harsh mystery~~

~~Death & life, or call it sweet Life in Death~~

Death in life, or that dear Life in Death

And I adore that mystery

Harsh death in life, or that dear life in death

                    an image   *man or shade*
Before me bends ~~a something, man or shade or man~~

Shade more than man, more image than a shade,

~~Treads on the intricate~~

~~And though it is all wound in mummy cloth~~

~~And though it seem all wound in mummy cloth~~

~~It treads on the intricate (   ) path;~~

~~And being wound in the intricate~~

~~And wound in the intricate mummy cloth~~

~~It knows the winding of the path~~

~~And though bodies~~ limbs are

What if the ~~limbs are~~ wound in mummy cloth

That know the winding of the path,

What if the bodies dry the mouths lack breath
        summons or beckons
That ~~beckons me summons~~ me

I adore that mystery

~~Called death in life, or~~

And call it death in life, or Life in Death

Below this he wrote in pencil:

That I call death in life

and again in pencil, along the left-hand edge of the page:

Limbs that have been bound in mummy cloth
                         a
~~May be~~ are more content with ~~the~~ winding path

> *A mouth that has no moisture & no breath*
>
> *May better summon me*
>
> *To adore*

Finally, there slants across the foot of the page:

> *I hail the superhuman,*
>
> *~~Or death in life~~*
>
> *And call it etc*

So stanza II grows round the nucleus of a Coleridgean image:

> The Nightmare Life-in-Death was she,
> Who thicks man's blood with cold.

On page 4 Yeats turns to stanza III, whose opening lines spring fully formed on to the paper. We know from his letter to Sturge Moore that he had been reconsidering the golden bird.

> *Miracle, bird or golden handy work*
>
> *More miracle than bird or handywork*
>
> *~~Sings to the starlight~~*
>
> *~~Set hidden by golden leaf~~*
>
> *(————)*
>   *and*
> *What ~~mighty~~ hand ~~or~~ imagined out of metal*
>
>
> *In scorn   stood   imbued*
> *In mockery of nature's blood & petal*
>
> *In mockery of nature's mire & blood*
>
> *In mockery   metal*
>
> *Mocking blind nature's mire & blood*
>
> *~~A great~~*
>
> *~~What great artificer~~*

~~What mind decreed or hammer shaped the metal,~~

~~Of golden~~

Elaborately crossing out with vertical strokes the previous lines, Yeats breaks free from the intrusive echoes of Blake's 'Tyger':

What the hammer? what the chain?
In what furnace was thy brain?

Suddenly, I think, the 'golden leaf' (of line 4 of this page) suggested to him the golden bough of mythology, and at once his pen is off on a new track:

~~Carrols~~ Mutters
~~Sings all~~ night long out of a golden bough

~~Or sings~~ What the birds of Hades know

~~Or roused by star or moonlight mocks~~
                                    scorns
~~Or wakened by the moonlight sings aloud~~
                                    wakened
Or by the star or moonlight mocks aloud

~~Under a golden or a silver petal~~

~~Under a golden~~
                                    In the changeless metal
~~Out of the glory of its changeless metal~~ A glory of ~~changeless metal~~

~~In mockery of leaf & petal~~   Living leaf or petal

~~Mockery of man~~   And man's intricacy of mire & blood

Because this ends the page, Yeats here turned the notebook round and consolidated his corrections along the right-hand edge:

~~or else by the stars or moon em~~

Mutters upon a starlight golden bough

What the birds of Hades know

Or by the moon embittered scorns aloud

In glory of changeless metal

Formerly the golden bird was 'roused by star or moonlight', but star and moon are now separated, and a further level of symbolic meaning is added to the lines. It seems to stand somewhere between the moon and the more remote stars. Embittered sometimes by the changing moon it looks back to the earth and

scorns aloud

In glory of changeless metal

Living leaf or petal.

At other times it will turn its back on these: then, when the golden bough is starli(gh)t, it shares the knowledge of the 'birds of Hades', that represent, as I suggested in the previous chapter, the souls of the departed. The golden bird, in other words, is 'skilled to sing of time and eternity'.

Page 5 begins with a sketch prose-draft of stanza IV:

And there is a certain square where tall flames wind and unwind

And in the flames dance spirits, by that their agony made pure

And though they are all folded up in flame

It cannot singe a sleeve

His guide in stanza III had shown him something of the ultimate Heaven-state, and now, beginning the return journey, brings him to the place of Purgatory. As several critics have pointed out, Yeats's source here was probably the Japanese Noh play *Motemezuka*, which is known to have made a great impression on him. A young girl's sins during life are punished by torment through flame in the Buddhist purgatory, and the play ends with 'the dance of her agony', which Yeats describes in an essay in *Visions And Beliefs In The West of Ireland*:

She had but to lay her hand upon a pillar to make it burst into flame; she was perpetually burning. The priest tells her that if she can but cease to believe in her punishments they will cease to exist. She listens in gratitude, but she cannot cease to believe, and while she is speaking they (her guilty scruples) come upon her and she rushes away enfolded in flames.

The striking objective detail in 'It cannot singe a sleeve', derives of course from the wide Japanese kimono sleeve.

The prose-draft in page 5 is followed by a rough verse-draft of the stanza:

> live
>
> ~~flame~~
>
> sleeve

> ~~Flames upon the marble~~
>
> ~~A flame on the cathedral pavement~~ flits
>
> At midnight on the marble pavement flits
>
> ~~A certain flame~~
>   fagot
> ~~Flames that no wood fuel feeds, no hand has lit~~
>   nor   nor taper
> A flame ~~that~~   fagot feeds, ~~no mortal~~ lights
>   Nor
> ~~No~~ breath of wind disturbs & to this that flame
>   Do ~~all the~~
> ~~Can May the unrighteous spirits come~~
>
> ~~And~~ May all unpurged spirits come
>
> And all their blood begotten passion leave
>
> ~~And the agony of a dance~~ agony of trance!
>
> That is a measured dance
>   Or
> ~~Or~~ agony of fire that cannot singe a sleeve!

'Of fire', in the last line, Yeats corrected in pencil to 'the flame'; and on page 6 pencilled a rough correction of two previous lines:

>   ~~All The~~
>   ~~May~~ may
> ~~All~~ blood besotted spirits come
>
>   ~~And all that blood's imagination leave,~~
>   the all
> And ~~all~~ blood's fury in that flame may leave

The action of this stanza takes place at midnight, which, being the moment when one day gives place to the next, fittingly represents death.[1] Here, for purgation, come the spirits of the newly dead. Their passions, and later they themselves, are described as 'blood begotten', an epithet whose ambiguity I take to be deliberate, for not only are the spirits begotten of flesh and blood but they are also heirs of violence (hence 'blood besotted'). Their agony is in the form of a dance, and not by accident did Yeats precede 'Byzantium' in *The Winding Stair* with 'Mohini Chatterjee', a poem which ends:

> Birth-hour and death-hour meet,
> Or, as great sages say,
> Men dance on deathless feet.

The dance, with its associations of controlled energy and intricate patterning, is one of his major symbols. It appears in *A Vision* as The Dance of the Four Royal Persons, which 'is one of the names for the first figure drawn by the Judwali elders for the instruction of youth and is identical with the "Great Wheel" of Giraldus'.[2] On page 8 begins the first draft of stanza IV:

> ~~A straddle on the dolphin's mire & blood~~
>
> ~~Come the thin shades~~
>
> ~~The~~
>
> ~~The blood besotted~~
>
> *A straddle on the dolphin's mire & blood*
>
> ~~Where the~~
>
> ~~Come spirits where~~
>   *The crowds*
> ~~These spirits~~ *approach ; the marble breaks the flood ;*
>
> ~~The lettered marble of the emperor ;~~
>   *pavement*
> ~~The enchanted marble of the emperor ;~~
>
> ~~Shadowy feet upon the floor,~~

Innumerable feet, passion heavy feet

~~*Intricacy of the dancing floor*~~

~~*The intricate pavement of the emperor,*~~

~~*Flame upon the dancing floor,*~~

~~*Simplicity*~~

The bronze & marble of the emperor,

Simplicity of the dancing floor ⸦,

~~*A crowd of spirits*~~

~~*Breaks*~~

~~*The fin tortured*~~

~~*The dolphin torn*~~

~~*The dolphin tortured tide breaks*~~

~~*That dolphin tortured flood breaks into spray*~~

~~*That gong tormented current breaks in spray in foam*~~

~~*The Dolphin torn, the gong tormented sea.*~~

The poet's guide, having shown him something of Paradise and Purgatory, brings him now to the harbour and one stage nearer life. Here they see 'fish that carry souls to Paradise', that subject which Yeats's diary tells us had been in his head for some time. Like the golden bird on the golden bough, the Emperor and the fires of purgation, the dolphins are only invested with their full imaginative potency in this second poem. Since they traffic between the shores of the natural and the supernatural worlds, they, like their riders, are compounded of 'mire & blood'. Sea and dolphins dominate the poet's mind at this stage, and it is fascinating to see him struggling towards the great image of the last line.

He carries the second half of the stanza a little nearer its completed state on page 7:

~~Breaks~~   *intricacy*
Breaks the bleak glittering ~~intricacy,~~

~~Breaks~~

                              ~~breaks into foam spray~~
                                   ~~Breaks~~

~~Blood blind images yet~~

~~Blood blind images that yet~~

~~Where blind images beget~~

~~Where the blind images beget~~
       Break   *that*
~~Where blind images can yet~~

~~Blinder images beget~~

~~The Dolphin torn, the gong tormented sea.~~

Where blind images can yet

Blinder images beget

The Dolphin torn & gong tormented sea.

The finished syntax of the last stanza is notoriously difficult, but this draft I believe holds the key to Yeats's meaning. The last lines not crossed out on page 8:

The bronze & marble of the emperor,

Simplicity of the dancing floor ⎬,

seem to be the subject of the verb 'Break'. At first he wrote, 'Simplicity . . . Breaks the bleak glittering intricacy'. Dissatisfied with this, he makes 'Blood blind images' and 'The Dolphin torn, the gong tormented sea' into the object of the verb. The 'Blood blind images', which are clearly the spirits of the newly dead, and the turbulent sea from which they come, are broken, checked, and 'changed utterly' when they reach 'The bronze & marble of the emperor'.

                    blind images that yet

          Blinder images beget

suggests the ceaseless influx of 'blood begotten spirits', each generation blinder than that from which it sprung. This interpretation,
I believe, applies equally well to the lines in their final form.

On page 10 the poem moves forward a stage into its first complete draft:

I

The unpurged
     ~~*loud*~~
~~*All the foul*~~ *images of day recede,*
     The emperor's drunken soldiers are
~~*Soldier, robber & victim are*~~ *a bed;*

Night's resonance recedes, night walker's song

After cathedral gong;

A starlit or a moonlit dome distains
     `\  \`
All that man is,
        mire
All ~~*the intricacies,*~~ *complexity ies*
        mire ~~*blood &*~~ *mire & blood*
All ~~*the mire & blood of*~~ *human veins*

II

          flits
Before me ~~*treads*~~ *an image, man, or shade*

Shade more than man, more image than a shade;
               bound
~~*An image that was wound in mummy cloth*~~
     ~~*Recalls or can recall*~~
~~*Best knows that winding path;*~~

~~*A mouth that has no moisture & no breath*~~
     ~~*Cries out the summons*~~
~~*Can stoutly summon*~~   ~~*Man's blood may can*~~
     ~~*Can merrily summon me*~~ ~~*Can all blood summon*~~
~~*I hail the superhuman*~~
     ~~+~~
~~*And*~~ *call it death in life or life in death.*

III

Miracle, bird, or golden handy work,

More miracle than bird or handy work,

~~Mutters upon a starlit golden bough~~ Planted on a starlit golden bough

~~All that the birds of Hades know~~ Can like the cocks of Hades crow

Or by the moon embittered scorn aloud
    ~~measured~~
~~In glory of changeless metal~~

~~Living leaf or petal,~~
  ~~Or blind, measureless imagery~~
~~And Man's intricacy of mire & blood.~~

IV

emperor's
At midnight on the ~~marble~~ pavement flits

A flame nor fagot feeds nor taper lights
    ~~To that flame~~
Nor breath disturbs, ~~a self begotten flame;~~
  ~~There~~
~~Images & spirits come, & to that flame born flame~~

~~Images and spirits come~~ a flame begotten flame
  ~~Where~~
~~All imaged spirits thither come~~

~~And There all their blood begotten fury leave~~

~~O agony of trance~~

~~That is a measured dance.~~

~~O agony of flame that cannot singe a sleeve.~~

For the moment I pass over page 9, with its corrections to three of these stanzas; and also page 11, which contains the prose draft of a letter. On page 12 there are two drafts of stanza V:

V

A straddle on the dolphins' mire & blood
  Those ~~images~~   metal
~~The~~ crowds approach; the ~~marble~~ breaks the flood;
  ~~Precious metals~~
~~The golden smithies of the emperor;~~
  ~~Simplicity integrity~~
~~Integrity of the dancing floor; integrity~~

~~Breaks the bleak glittering intricacies aimless flood of imagery~~

     that
   Where~~ Images ~~can~~ yet

  More images beget
       that gong
  That ~~golphin~~ Dolphin torn, ~~& gong~~ tormented sea

Below this there is a correction of lines 35, 36, and 37:

  The precious metal of the emperor;

  Marble of the dancing floor

  Breaks that ~~bitter bleak complexity~~
     bright flood, that bleak complexity

Yeats then wrote the date, 11 June (1930), and followed this with another draft of the stanza:

  A straddle on the Dolphins' mire & blood

  Those crowds approach; smithys break the flood,

  The golden smithys of the emperor;

  Marbles of the Dancing floor

  Break bleak bitter, bleak, aimless complexity,

  Those images that yet

  More images beget

  That dolphin torn, that gong tormented sea.

 This complete draft of the poem shows an immense advance on the preliminary fragments that preceded it: hardly a line has not been tightened and compressed. From stanza I the 'I' figure of the poet has been removed, and every objective detail that remains makes a contribution to the dominant theme. The cathedral gong sounds like the last heartbeat of a dying man, and at once all other noises fade. As we move away from the natural world, our attention is directed to 'A starlit or a moonlit dome', which can be either, or both, that of St. Sophia and/or the wider dome of heaven. The ambiguity is surely deliberate, and the suggestion of double vision is brilliantly in keeping with that of a dying man.

The clean simplicity of the dome ahead makes a striking contrast with the foul, drunken, violent complexities that are being left behind.

Stanza II has also been trimmed and compressed, and the word 'Intricate' abandoned. In stanza IV, the lines:

> *Mutters upon a starlit golden bough*
>
> *All that the birds of Hades know*

are changed to:

> *Planted on a starlit golden bough*
>
> *Can like the cocks of Hades crow.*

'Birds of Hades' become 'cocks of Hades', because the cock, which crows for sunrise, is an old Resurrection symbol; used by Vaughan in his poem 'Cock Crowing' and by Yeats himself in *The Dreaming of the Bones*. In stanza IV, what was once 'the cathedral pavement' is now 'the emperor's pavement', and the flames are now 'flame begotten'.

The greatest additions and alterations, however, are to the last stanza. For the first time 'smithys break the flood': the prototypes of these celestial craftsmen are to be found, I suggest, in the *Rosa Alchemica*, which Yeats had written as long ago as 1877:

. . . it seemed to my troubled fancy that all those little points of light filling the sky were the furnaces of innumerable divine alchemists, who labour continually, turning lead into gold, weariness into ecstasy, bodies into souls.

So in his vision of 1930, the smithies turn lead (or dross) into gold, weariness into ecstasy, bodies into souls. They, like the bird on the golden bough, are described as golden, because that had been the metal of the gods and their possessions since the Greeks wrote of 'Golden Aphrodite' and 'the golden horses of Poseidon'.

In this draft the last line is transformed by the repeated demonstrative adjective so much more powerful than the old definite article: 'That dolphin torn, that gong tormented sea.' In this magnificent climax is epitomized the conflict central to 'Byzantium', of death-wish and the terror of death. The sea of life and

passion is torn by the joyful dolphins, and tormented by the gong
of doom. Alliteration instantly sets dolphin and gong in opposition
to one another. In 'Sailing to Byzantium' Yeats was far enough
from death to regard it as 'a consummation devoutly to be wished',
but 'Byzantium'—as its shorter lines, swifter and more subtle
rhythms imply—is a more complex and profound poem. Attraction and repulsion between them generate a most passionate intensity.

I return now to page 9, with its corrections of stanzas II, III,
and IV, which are linked to the relevant lines on page 10 by
swerving arrows.

> ~~Hades a bobbin~~ *For Hades' bobbin*
> ~~A bobbin that is~~ *bound in mummy cloth*
> *May unwind*
> ~~Can unravel~~ *the winding path*
>
> *A mouth that has no moisture & no breath*
>
> *Breathing mouths may summon—*
>
> *I hail the superhuman*
>
>
> ~~Can best Unbinds the bobbin of the path~~
>
> ~~All a breathing mouth can~~
>
> ~~All breathing clay~~
>
> ~~Mire & blood can summon~~

The addition of 'Hades bobbin' and 'Breathing mouths' brings
stanza II a notable step nearer completion. Although 'Breathing
mouths' later became 'Breathless mouths', in both cases I think
Yeats meant that *his* mouth—he was poised, for the purposes of
the poem, between life and death—was able to summon his ghostly
guide.

There is an improvement to stanza III (lines 22–24):

> ~~all that~~ *glory of changeless*
> ~~In all simplicity~~ *of metal*
> *or leaf*
> ~~Common Bird or petal~~

~~Living leaf or petal~~

~~And Every complexity of mire & blood~~

Common bird or petal

And all complexities of mire or blood

and a further improvement to stanza IV (lines 28–32):

    Where
    ~~There~~
~~Where~~ blood begotten spirits come

And   *All complexities of fury leave*

Dying into a dance

An agony of trance
    An
~~And~~ agony of flame that cannot singe a sleeve.

On page 14 begins the final manuscript draft, where for the first time appears the poem's title:

Byzantium
I
The unpurged images of day recede;

The emperor's drunken soldiery are a bed;

Night's resonance recedes, ~~&~~ night-walker's song
   ~~And that the great~~   After great
After cathedral gong,

A starlit or a moonlit dome distains
   \   \
All that man is,

All mere complexities,
   ~~That stupidity and~~
~~All mere~~ mire ~~& blood~~ of human veins

The fury and the

II
Before me floats an image, man or shade,

Shade more than man, more image than a shade;

For Hades' bobbin bound in mummy cloth

May unwind the winding path;

A mouth that has no moisture & no breath

Breathing mouths may summon.

I hail the superhuman;

I call it death in life or life in death.

III

Miracle, bird, or golden handy-work,

More miracle than bird or handy-work,

Planted on a starlit golden bough,

Can like the cocks of Hades crow,

Or by the moon embittered scorn aloud,

In glory of changeless metal,

Common bird or petal

And all complexities of mire or blood.

IV

At midnight on the emperor's pavement flits
A flame nor ~~fagot~~ feeds nor taper lights faggot

Nor breath disturbs, a flame begotten flame,

Where blood begotten spirits come

And all complexities of fury leave,

Dying into a dance,

An agony of trance,

An agony of flame that cannot singe a sleeve.

The final stanza is on page 13:

> ~~a straddle on~~

> V

> *A straddle on the dolphins' mire & blood*

> *Those crowds approach; smithys break the flood,*
>   *smithys*
> *The golden ~~smithys~~ of the emperor;*

> *Marbles of the dancing floor*
>   ~~*stupid aimless furies of*~~
> ~~*Break bitter, bleak, aimless complexity,*~~
>   *aimless*
> *Those images that yet*
>   ~~*Fresh*~~ *More*
> ~~*More*~~ *images beget,*

> *That dolphin torn, that gong tormented sea.*

Below this a swirling arrow links a correction to the relevant point
in the stanza:

> ~~*Break the bleak fury of or blind complexity*~~

> ~~*Of images that yet*~~

> ~~*Fresh images beget*~~
>   *bitter*
> *Break, ~~bleak, blind~~ furies of complexity*

> *Those images that yet*

> *Fresh images beget*

This draft shows only a few changes. In line 2, 'soldiers' is altered
to the less precise and more symbolic 'soldiery'; 'great' is added to
'cathedral gong' to fill out line 4; and lines 37 and 39 are fixed in
their final shape. There are two loose folios of manuscript that
show all but one of the significant changes incorporated at the
poem's first printing. 'Breathing mouths' in line 14 has still to be
altered to 'Breathless mouths', thereby tightening the link with
line 13; but Yeats has sharpened the focus on his image in line 19

by changing 'a' to ' "the" starlit golden bough'. Lines 25–27 become in this draft:

> At midnight on the emperor's pavement flits̶
> feeds ̶t̶h̶a̶t̶ nor steel has lit
> Flames that no fagot ̶n̶o̶u̶r̶i̶s̶h̶e̶s̶,̶ ̶n̶o̶ ̶s̶t̶e̶e̶l̶ ̶l̶i̶g̶h̶t̶s̶
>
> Nor storm disturbs, flames begotten of flame,

and the torrential movement of the last stanza is sustained much better by 'Spirit after spirit!' than by the rather tame statement: 'Those crowds approach;' in line 34.

Considered together, the drafts of 'Sailing to Byzantium' and 'Byzantium' reveal the growth of what is almost a single poem. The themes at least are the same, though, properly, they are examined with greater vision and technical dexterity in the second part: but whether considered separately or together they triumphantly survive the severest test to which poetry can be subjected. No matter from what angle one approaches Yeats's Byzantium, and many critics have travelled by many different routes, its magic and mystery defy definition, and at every point one is aware of other levels and areas of meaning, still unexplored, just beyond the range of sight.

VII

CHOSEN

••

 1. The lot of love is chosen. I learnt that much
 2. Struggling for an image on the track
 3. Of the whirling Zodiac.
 4. Scarce did he my body touch,
 5. Scarce sank he from the west
 6. Or found a subterranean rest
 7. On the maternal midnight of my breast
 8. Before I had marked him on his northern way,
 9. And seemed to stand although in bed I lay.

10. I struggled with the horror of daybreak,
11. I chose it for my lot! If questioned on
12. My utmost pleasure with a man
13. By some new-married bride, I take
14. That stillness for a theme
15. Where his heart my heart did seem
16. And both adrift on the miraculous stream
17. Where—wrote a learned astrologer—
18. The Zodiac is changed into a sphere.

PARTING

1. *He.* Dear, I must be gone
2. While night shuts the eyes
3. Of the household spies;
4. That song announces dawn.

5. *She.* No, night's bird and love's
6. Bids all true lovers rest,
7. While his loud song reproves
8. The murderous stealth of day.

9. *He.* Daylight already flies
10. From mountain crest to crest.

11. *She.* That light is from the moon.

12. *He.* That bird . . .

    She.   Let him sing on,
13. I offer to love's play
14. My dark declivities.

ON the dating of the lyrical sequence entitled 'A Woman Young and Old' there has been some disagreement among the critics. Jeffares[1] and Hone[2] favour 1926, while Ellmann, dating the poems individually, assigns some of them to 1927. This is not a matter of major importance: indeed, dates can seldom be more than approximately fixed. The poet himself might even find it difficult. Is he to record the day when he first set pen to paper; when he completed the first draft; or when he corrected the final comma in the final proof?

This is by way of prologue to an examination of 'Chosen' and 'Parting', which Ellmann dates differently. 'Chosen' he believes to have been written in 1927,[3] and 'Parting' in August 1926.[4] In the case of one, at least, he must be wrong, since the manuscripts show them to have been written at the same time: more than this, they show them to have been originally parts of the same poem.

For once I begin my examination with a typescript fragment. It would seem to have been intended as an explanatory footnote, and certainly it is an illuminating introduction to the two poems:

. . . In 'A First Confession', 'The Choice' and 'The Parting' I have made use of that symbolic marriage of the Sun and Light with the Earth and Darkness, current in literature since the Renaissance. The sun's northern (not northward) way is his passage under the earth, his sojourn in the bed of love. Earth would bar his way and so prevent the dawn. ~~It was in Blake at times the symbol of the grave.~~

~~'He who shall train the horse to war~~

~~Shall never pass the Polar Bar.'~~

[1] *W. B. Yeats/Man and Poet*, 1949, p. 246.
[2] *W. B. Yeats/1865–1939*, 1942, p. 372.
[3] *Yeats/The Man and the Masks*, 1949, p. 264.
[4] *The Identity of Yeats*, 1954, p. 293.

'Chosen' (originally 'The Choice') and 'Parting' appear to have been conceived as parts of a much longer poem entitled 'Two Voices'. The two voices are, of course, those of a man and a woman, or the sun and the earth. A preliminary dialogue (parts 1–4) which takes place as the night of love hurries to its close, is in the tradition of the aubade: this is followed (part 5) by a soliloquy from the woman who, as 'an old hag with speckled shin', looks into 'The dark backward and abysm of time.'

The manuscript is scattered over eleven loose sheets and twenty-five pages of a green-lined exercise book: there is also one typescript of 'Parting'. It would seem that Yeats wrote 'Two Voices' in two parts; 1–4 and 5. The manuscript, however, gives no clue as to which was written first, so I have assumed that Yeats followed the order in which they appear in the first fair copy. F. 1r reads:

Two Voices

He

To a visionary eye
~~Armed men out of Heaven's gate~~
~~Light bursts upon the eastern sky~~
~~all~~   ~~Heaven calls up its armoured~~ men,
~~And each armoured heavenly man~~
~~To~~   armoured men from Heaven's gate
Gallops towards

~~The night disordered hordes~~

~~The dark night's broken hordes~~
    ~~The~~ un
~~The~~ night's broken hordes
            ~~clanging~~
Harken to the ~~clanging~~ swords   ringing|
                        Are not love & enmity
~~For each has found that enemy~~
                    Predestinate
~~Predestined when the world began.~~

She.

No clanging swords but everywhere
    Heaven (   ) upon the wing
~~Birds are upon (   ) birds are upon the wing~~

~~A multitude upon the wing~~

And that sweet sound

Shows that each bird has found

That heart whereto its heart is bound

~~In furthest shadow on bright air~~

~~And~~ In shadow or in brightening air

And all delighted sing

He

    all are
~~When~~ A ~~man well~~ mounted & hand

~~Practised in feats of~~

Practice has made deft & strong

For every hilt

Who thinks of blood new spilt

Of this draft, all but the man's first speech has been cancelled by a diagonal line, and on F. 2r Yeats continued with what, somewhat altered, was to be the beginning of 'Two Voices' in the fair copy:

He

~~Time that I was rode~~
    dare not stay
Love I ~~must away:~~
    Night shuts   Night still ~~ha~~ shuts the eyes
~~Night still shuts the eyes~~ Night ~~shadows still~~ the eyes

Of the household spies

But that shrill skylark has announced the day

She

    nightingale
A ~~nightingale~~ that sings

In starts of sudden song

Till all the garden rings!

For love's throat is strong

~~And~~ *How could that belong*

To the murderous day

He

    ~~The The~~ *s*
~~The~~ *casement glimmers grey*

She

    Love's great moon's leaped from the mountain side

~~That pale~~   ~~A silvery crescent clears the~~

   ~~The moon this horn has left the~~ *mountain side.*
*   *leaps*
*   ~~A horned moon springs from the mountain side~~

He

~~That brightness is the day~~   ~~Night's shadow~~ *must away*
   The room is grown   ~~The chamber~~
~~Room grows~~ *bright with day*   ~~The shadows~~ *flee away—*
                     Love's dark has fled away
                     Love's ~~great night has fled~~
                     dark has fled away

She

Come what brightness may

                      ~~hide~~
Between these breasts maternal ~~shadows hides hid~~

dark ~~night~~ *lies hid.*
          ~~dark (   ) hide.~~
    ~~And night has lies hid hid~~
       ~~had is hid has hid~~

This part of the poem was eventually to be detached from the rest, under the title of 'Parting'. The source-hunters have here, I think, been unnecessarily busy. Saul suggests that Walther von der Vogelweide's 'Song at Daybreak', Swinburne's 'In the Orchard', and Pound's 'Alba Innominata' and 'Langue D'Oc', may have

---

* Denotes a line inserted from the foot of the page.

been at the back of Yeats's mind. Hone is probably nearer the
mark when he glosses *Romeo and Juliet*, Act II, scene v: Shakespeare's lovers share the uncertainty over lark or nightingale, and
in each case it is the woman who argues for the latter. The obvious
echoes of 'Hark, hark, the lark At Heaven's gate sings', on F. 1*r*,
support the case for Shakespearian influence. One other clear echo
can be followed to its source, and I owe its detection to Miss Helen
Gardner. The phrase 'household spies', which persists in the poem
from its earliest draft, Yeats either assimilated from his reading
of Donne's 'Twelfth Elegy' (in Grierson's 1912 edition), or, less
probably, of Ben Jonson's *Volpone*, Act III, scene v.

F. 3*r* is a small sheet of notepaper. The woman speaks:

II

>   *is its setting*
> *Love's morning's a forgetting*
>   *All*
> *And though all night it burn,*
>
> *   *All night its memories burn*
>
> *   *But day is foul forgetting.*
>   *The day is mere*
> *Day is its forgetting*
>
> *And what and if dark*
>   *its dark*
> *If dark night's dark noon return*
>
> *That is no great defiance*
>   *From Turks & blackamores*
> *For Turks & blackamores*
>
> *And Abyssinian lions,*
>
> *African warriors*
>   *A   winding*
> *The dragon's rolling gullet*
>
> *That has sucked in the moon*
>   *Rage   tusk*
> *Raging tooth, tusk & bullet*

* Denotes a line inserted from the foot of the page.

       be
    ~~Till passion's race is run~~

    ~~Although all true love~~

    ~~And good faith is undone~~

    ~~Keep true love from its noon~~

    ~~To~~

    ~~To drive true love from its noon.~~

    To drive it from its noon

On F. 4*r* the man replies:

       He
    Lift that love bewildered eye

    Morning is at Heaven's gate

    And gallops towards

    The night's unbroken hordes

    Harken to the ringing swords

    Are not love & enmity

    Predestinate.
       She
      Kiss me for I hear the song
    ~~One kiss the more   I hear the song~~

~~of~~   ~~The casement's open is open to song~~
      Many a happy climbing wing
  Of ~~good luck on climbing~~ *wing*

    All have found

    Hearts to travel round

    In their labyrinth of sound

    And that is why their throats are strong

    And the clouds ring

F. 4*v*:   *He*

      Nothing can be strong but war
      ~~*When men are mounted for the war*~~
         ~~*When*~~ *a*
      ~~*Every*~~ *rider's practised hand*
         Is on
      ~~*Griping*~~ *the hilt*
         Who
      ~~*Now*~~ *measure guilt*
         Or   the
      Mutters of blood new spilt

      If metal ring on metal there

      The Heavens have planned.

              She

      Lost in
      ~~*Out of*~~ *Heaven's oblivion*
      Those angels wantons
      ~~*The wanton (*~~   *)* ~~*falls to*~~ *bless*

      The attentive ear

      And hang a happy tear

      Ever on faces ~~*that are*~~ *blanched with fear*

      ~~*Stop yet a while*~~
         ~~*And (*~~   ~~*) is done*~~
      ~~*That (*~~   ~~*) is not done*~~
         ~~*In idleness*~~
      O heart lie close where all that's done

      Is idleness

This page takes over so much from F. 1*r* that I think Yeats must have already abandoned it.

At this point he turned his attention to Part V (afterwards entitled 'Chosen'), beginning on F. 5*r* with a rapidly scribbled prose draft:

      ~~*It*~~
      He has gone forth—out to danger of of the

      ~~*murderous (*~~   ~~*) men*~~

> *murderous day—day all things are full*
>
> *of herald—cry here between my breasts*
>
> *is it safe—(   ) men, the*
>
> *great sea, the shadows sea. O my*
>
> *beloved (   ) to long*
>
> *hence will sit alone by fire & recall*
>
> *this night—(   ) will cry out*
>
> *~~to moments peace, satisfied love~~*
>
> *~~that~~ the night long (   )*
>
> *the lip could go & come.*

The woman who here passionately addresses her lover has not yet been identified with the earth. She speaks of present love and of that future night, when,

> *. . . old and grey and full of sleep*
> *And nodding by the fire,*

she will recall her one brief hour of satisfied love. In his lifelong exploration of the nature of love Yeats several times assumed the mask of the woman: 'A Cradle Song', for instance, he had written as long ago as 1890.

Here, having written his prose draft, he would seem to have snatched up two loose end-papers of his book, *A Vision* (1925), which had originally been sent to him for signature. On both he wrote on the reverse, swiftly and impatiently, crossing out and over-writing his corrections so densely that only a few sentences are legible. From F. 6*v* I can salvage:

> *could in safety*
> *He ~~lay a~~ while at rest*
>
> *Here in passion's eagle nest . . .*
>
> *In the shadow of my breast he . . .*
>
> *When the sun sank in the west*

Passion found . . .

Among the living shadow of my breast . . .

Now he has sprung into an eagle's nest . . .

The use of 'sun' and 'west' I think suggests that the poet has already in mind the macrocosmic level of meaning to his poem. On F. 7v he wrestles with his first two lines, exploring the idea of death/murder/day: these three words recur again and again. At this point he reached for a sheet of notepaper (F. 8r) headed 82, Merrion Square, Dublin, and wrote—a little more legibly:

Though (   ) death
            mixed our breath

~~*I thought the*~~

~~*I thought that mind & heart come again*~~

~~*And now*~~

~~*But know now that he will be slain*~~

~~*I know—I now where we first mixed our breath*~~
   I know where   meet his death
   I knew that would change or ~~meet~~
      love's midnight
Before ~~that midnight~~ had come round again—

~~*He had*~~

~~*Scarce had he*~~
   ~~*Scarce had his body by my body*~~ *lain*
~~*Sc*~~   *Body had scarce by body lain*

~~*And scarce had he on the west*~~ *west*

~~*Found*~~ *Breath had scarce been*
       mixed with breath

Slowly the thoughts begin to take order. Death and the moment of love are identified, following the well-established Elizabethan conceit: 'love's midnight' is consistent with Yeats's habitual use of midnight to indicate the precise moment of death; as in

   At stroke of midnight soul cannot endure
   A bodily or mental furniture.

He continues with this theme on F. 8*v*:

> ~~For he~~
>   *west*
> ~~Scarce had he on this found~~
>
> ~~Found subterranean~~
>
> Scarce had he found his west
>
> Her subterranean rest
>
> Amid amongst my shadows in the west
>
> ~~Be I knew he travelled south~~
>
> Before I knew
>   *he trod the southern way*
>   ~~While~~
> And I stood still though in one bed we lay

The human act of love is now clearly conceived in terms of the astronomical metaphor. The unhelpful pun 'trod' is dropped on F. 5*v* where stanza I as a whole is advanced a stage further:

> *III*
> I knew that he would
>   *change or meet his death*
> ~~Before love's midnight could come round again~~
>
> Before my shadows could be filled again
>   ~~When~~
> ~~Scarce~~ body had scarce by body lain.
>   *scarce had been*
> Breath ~~had scarce~~ been mixed in breath
>
> Scarce had he ~~moved~~ found the west
>
> ~~Or sunk in subterranean rest~~
>
> ~~Among the ivory shadow of this rest~~
>   ~~him on the southern way~~
> ~~Before I marked his passage to the south~~
>
> And I stood stock still, though on our bed we lay
>
>
> Among the shadows of my breast
>
> When brooding on the subterranean rest

I marked his passage on the southern way

And stood stock still though in our bed we lay

F. 9r is headed 82, Merrion Square, Dublin, and began as a letter to 'Dear Mrs Parkington'. It is dated 'Jan. 25', which would seem to support Ellmann's theory that this poem was written early in 1927. The stanza now has a definite shape:

Never, never will he come again

For he will change, or somewhere meet his death.

Scarce had breath been mixed in breath
~~Scarce were we two~~
Scarce had one with tother lain

That he might find his west

And sink in subterranean rest

Among the ivory shadows of my breast

Before I'd marked him on the southern way

And stood stock still though in our bed we lay.

The chief additions here are the opening, which would seem to be an unconscious recollection of Lear's

> . . . She'll come no more,
> Never, never, never, never, never.

and the near-oxymoron of 'ivory shadows'.

Yeats begins stanza II on a sheet of notepaper (F. 10r) headed Irish Federation of Arts. Here, and later in the exercise book, he uses both ink and pencil: the latter I transcribe in bold italic. The jottings on F. 10r begin with a geometrical image.

whorl
~~I and my my broken circle in days long hence~~

~~Shall~~

> on a day long hence
When I—a broken circle— on ye

Shall count

Shall brood upon upon my joys & count them up

That night shall be a cup

Wherein all all sup, &

Where (————)

Wherein all life's lost exuberance

Flow until it

It finds its

Here the pencilled workings begin:

When I
> in a ( ) long hence
I shall sit sit crouched
> *When I an old hag warm a speckled shin*
When I shall crouch in a great chair long
And measure And count all my life's memories up
(————), and count my memories up
> as it were
This night shall seem a cup

When life all life's exuberance
Made round
Made round (————) memory deaf wherein

All that did so fill

That all your skill That found in life (————)

> *And in its own delight ( ) still*

Then, slanting along the right-hand edge of the page, he wrote:

All life seemed

So did my folly dream until

It found this shining river

Nature's whorl became a sphere

Yeats now turned to the exercise book, the numbering of whose pages I have kept distinct from that of the loose sheets. On the fly-leaf he continued to work at stanza II. The 'old hag with speckled shin' opens her soliloquy:

When I have reckoned up all good & ill

and after seven faint, crossed-out lines, she concludes:

I have dreamed that all others stood still

That I dreamed that we stood so still

It seemed upon the sky now chill

Nature The bitter zodiac changed to a sphere.

T. R. Henn suggests that the 'origin of the obscure cosmic image' may be in the Thirteenth Cycle of the Great Year.[1] Certainly this may have been at the back of Yeats's mind, but a less complicated interpretation he offers in a footnote:

> I have symbolized a woman's love as the struggle of the darkness to keep the sun from rising from its earthly bed. In the last stanza of The Choice I change the symbol to that of the souls of man and woman ascending through the Zodiac. In some Neo-Platonist or Hermatist—whose name I forget—the whorl changes into a sphere at one of the points where the Milky Way crosses the Zodiac.[2]

This again he expands in a Preface to *The Winding Stair and Other Poems*:

> The 'learned astrologer' in *Chosen* was Macrobius, and the particular passage was found for me by Dr. Sturm, that too little known poet and mystic. It is from Macrobius' comment upon 'Scipio's Dream' (Lib. I. Cap. XII, Sec. 5): '. . . when the sun is in Aquarius, we sacrifice to the Shades, for it is in the sign inimical to human life; and from thence the meeting-place of Zodiac and Milky Way, the descending soul by its defluction is drawn out of the spherical, the sole divine form into the cone.'[3]

At 'love's midnight' conflict is momentarily succeeded by harmony, antithesis is resolved in synthesis, and 'the whorl changes into a sphere'—'the sole divine form'. 'Whorl' and 'gyre' are the same for

---

[1] *The Lonely Tower*, 1950, p. 188.
[2] *Variorum*, p. 830.   [3] Ibid., p. 831.

Yeats, and explaining in *A Vision* his complex symbolism of the inter-penetrating gyres, he had written:

I see the Lunar and Solar cones first, before they start their whirling movement, as two worlds lying one within another—nothing exterior, nothing interior, Sun in Moon and Moon in Sun—a single being like man and woman in Plato's Myth, and then a separation and a whirling for countless ages, and I see man and woman as reflecting the greater movement, each with zodiac, precession, and separate measure of time, and all whirling perpetually.[1]

The sexual interpretation is made explicit in an unpublished poem that ends:

> *In love's levelling bed*
>
> *All gyres lie still.*

The lovers' union is then perfect and complete. In this preliminary draft of 'Chosen' the Zodiac is 'bitter', because 'the sun . . . is in the sign inimical to human life'. Hence (on F. 9*r*) the line: 'For he will change, or somewhere meet his death.'

On page 1 of the exercise book Yeats (in pencil) tries a different opening for the old woman's soliloquy:

> ~~*When I rock to & fro counting my treasures up*~~
>
> ~~*Or*~~
>
> ~~*When I grow old*~~
>
> ~~*When I grown old count all my memories up*~~
>
> *When the day comes to count my treasures up*
>
> *And rock my body, & warm a withered shin*
>
> ~~*I shall know what lie within*~~
>
> ~~*These nights*~~   *And know that all life lay*
>
> ~~*I shall cry out*~~   ~~*recall what lay*~~ *within*
>   *midnight's*
> ~~*On A night's deep*~~ *overflowing cup*

---

[1] 1925 edition, p. 149.

~~How~~

~~And seemed~~ seeming to stand still

For there was nothing more it could fill

And yet I let

Page 2 of the exercise book is blank, there are rough jottings on page 3, and the draft of this stanza on page 4, being a much later version (written in ink), must await its chronological turn. On page 5 the stanza begins to take a definite shape.

~~When I am old & all is reckoned up~~

~~I shall declare (────────────) good~~

~~Circled round & whirled~~

~~I shall declare when I have reckoned up~~

When on my death bed I have reckoned up

What ever I have known of the world's good

I shall declare it flowed
      Into one mid
~~In one deep~~ night's hollow cup

~~And did that cup so fill~~

And (──────) ~~& stood~~ still

~~For there~~ the

And did that cup so fill

~~It seemed that it stood still~~

It seemed as though all life stood still

~~So full of its own~~

Being too full of its own sweet to ~~still~~ spill

~~And~~

And that I played in starry waters where

The natural ~~whirl~~ whorl is changed into a sphere

Here, for the moment, Yeats left Part IV, and on page 7 began his fair copy of the complete poem:

Morning

I

He

Love I dare not stay

Night still shuts the eyes

Of the household spies

But the shrill skylark has announced the day

She

A nightingale that sings

In starts of sudden song

Till all the garden rings

For love's throat is strong.

How could that belong

To the murderous day.

He

The casement glimmers grey

She

Love's great moon's leaped from the mountain side.

He

Love's dark has fled away

She

Come what brightness may

Between these breasts maternal dark lies hid.

Page 9:   *II*

She

Love's morning is its setting

All night its memories burn

But day is foul forgetting

And if night's noon return

That is a great defiance,

For Turks & blackamores

Abbysinian lions,

Indian warriors,

A dragon's winding gullet

That has sucked in the moon,

Rage tooth tusk & bullet

To drive it from its noon.

                   III

He

Lift that love bewildered eye

Morning is at Heaven's gate

And gallops towards

The night's unbroken ~~hoards~~ hordes

Hark to the ringing swords

Are not love & enmity

Predestinate.

Page 11:

She

Kiss me for I hear the song

Of many a happy climbing wing

All have found

Hearts to travel round

In their labyrinthe of sound

And that is why their throats are strong

And the clouds ring.

He

Nothing can be strong but war

When a rider's practised hand

Is on the hilt

Who measures guilt

Or mutters of the blood new spilt

If metal ring on metal there

The heavens have planned.

She

Lost in heaven's oblivion

Those angels wantons bless

The attentive ear

And hang a happy tear

Ever on faces blenched with fear

O heart lie close where all that's done

Is idleness.

On page 13 the woman looks back, as yet from no great distance, at the one, brief night of love.

IV

She

I knew that he would change & meet his death—

Before my shadows could be filled again

Body had scarce by body lain

Breath scarce had mixed with breath—

Scarce had he found his west

Among the shadows of my breast

When brooding on the subterranean rest

I marked his passage on the southern way

And stood stock still though in my bed we lay

Yeats, dissatisfied, crossed this stanza out, and began again:

She

Love sets at dawn her door ajar
Never, never will he come again

For he will change or somewhere meet his death

Scarce had breath been mixed in breath

Scarce had one with tother lain

That he might find his ~~*rest*~~ *west*

And sink in sublunar rest

Among the ivory shadows of breast

northern
Before I'd marked him on his ~~*southern*~~ *way*

And stood stock still though in one bed we lay.

As he drafts the next stanza, Yeats alters his angle of vision and makes the woman look forward in time rather than backward as before.

> When on my death bed I have reckoned up
>
> Whatever I have known of the world's good
> > my strong
> For all strong nature would not stop
> > For Yet when grown I
> Yet when an old hag measures all the joy (   )

Page 15:

> I shall declare it flowed
>
> Into one midnight's hollow cup
>
> And did that cup so fill
>
> It seemed as though all life stood still
>
> Being too full of its own sweet to spill
>
> And that I played in starry waters where
>
> The zodiac is changed into a sphere

Abandoning the sexual symbolism of cup and starry waters, he begins once again in the first person:

> And yet grown old & cold I'll

before switching to the third person:

> No matter how material darkness stain
> > could
> His play mate is not severed from his track
>
> Upon the whirling zodiac
>
> For scarce had one by tother lain
>
> That he might find, &c.

At this point I think Yeats turned back to page 4 and there wrote:

> When on my death bed I have reckoned up
>
> Whatever I have known of the world's good

I shall declare it flowed

Into one night's hollow cup

And did that cup so fill

It seemed as though all life stood still

Being too full of its own sweet to spill

And that I played in starry waters where

The natural whirl is changed into a sphere.

Still not content, he turned the exercise book on its side and, writing rapidly across the lines, filled pages 16–23 with rough jottings. These culminate in a stanza on page 25.

famous
I shall be ~~questioned~~ for a story's sake

When old & cold & may be questioned on

My utmost pleasure with a man

By some new married bride I take
stillness for
~~That moment~~ for a theme
        ~~the other~~ tother
When the one (   ) ~~tother~~ seem
        miraculous
And both adrift ~~upon~~ on that ~~merridean~~ stream

That the great unicorn drinks up & there

Changed by dippipping to a single sphere

At once he revises the last three lines:

        ? meridian
As though a drop upon that glittering stream

Drunk by the famous unicorn & there

Changed by dipping to a single sphere

This is the last time 'Chosen' appears in the exercise book, but there is a later manuscript draft of the two stanzas on a sheet of typing-paper:

> *I know man's treacherous heart—I learned that much*
>
> ~~*By*~~ *Straining at an image on the track*
>
> *Of the whirling zodeac;*
>
> ~~*Scarce did body body touch*~~   *Scarce did he my body touch*
>
> ~~*Scarce fell he from the west*~~   *Scarce declined he from the west*
>
> *And found a subterranean rest*   *Or found a subterranean rest*
>
> *On the elaborate midnight of my breast*
>   *I had*
> *Before* ~~*I'd marked*~~ *him on his northern way*
>
> *And strained against him though in bed I lay.*

>   *day*
> ~~*Foreknowledge of the desolate year awoke;*~~
>   ~~*It seemed I chose my lot;*~~
>   *but*
> ~~*My heart became his heart—if questioned on*~~
>
> *My utmost pleasure with a man*
>
> *By some new married bride I take*
>
> *That stillness for a theme*
>   ~~*fellow*~~
> ~~*Where*~~   ~~*its fellow seem*~~ *My heart his heart did seem*
>
> *And both a drop on the miraculous stream*
>
> *That the great Unicorn drinks up & there,*
>
> *Drowning, transfigured to a single sphere.*

A swooping arrow from the first line of the second stanza indicates some later corrections:

>   *And after that*
> ~~*It seemed I had*~~ *foreknowledge of day break*
>   *The misery to come*
> ~~*And all that misery*~~: *but questioned on*
>   ~~*And after all that misery!*~~
> *And the day's misery.*

In these later drafts Yeats introduces a note of bitterness to the woman's recollections, as if to balance the brief but transcendental ecstasy of her experience. She speaks of 'man's treacherous heart', and has 'foreknowledge of day break And all that misery:'.

The astronomical 'image' now begins to define and illuminate the poem's central experience. The 'whirling zodiac' turns as inexorably as the wheel of Fortune, and the 'stillness' we know to be an illusion.

> *My heart his heart did seem*
>
> *And both a drop on the miraculous stream*

Seeming is not reality. 'The miraculous stream' is, on a literal level, the Milky Way, and on a symbolic level, I suggest, a sexual image like that found in the draft on page 158. 'The great Unicorn' is, of course, that constellation near the belt of Orion, which, stationed at the northern end of the Milky Way, seems to be drinking it.

By this stage 'Two Voices', the single poem, must have been divided into two poems, and parts II and III set aside, if not abandoned altogether. It is not difficult to see why. Dramatic dialogue has lapsed into sterile debate: the lovers talk almost at cross-purposes, the woman of love and the man of war. The verse movement reflects the triviality of its substance, as it runs on, endeavouring vainly to disguise the lack of tenderness and all conviction with a more romantic vocabulary ('Turks & blacka-mores', 'dragon', and 'angels'). Having cut out the centre of his poem, Yeats for no apparent reason reversed the beginning and the end. We have no typescript of 'Chosen', so must look to the printed text for the final changes.

The poem is now much more tightly knit. Important words are stressed by repetition—'lot', 'chose(n)', 'struggling/ed', for ex-ample, in the first two lines of each stanza. The rapid verse move-ment of stanza I admirably suggests the swift advance of 'Time's winged chariot', but this in line 14 is dramatically checked by the slow sibilants of 'stillness'. So nightmare is superseded by ecstasy. The unicorn has vanished and the zodiac been reintroduced to give the poetic argument a fuller symmetry.

There is an interesting typescript of part I of the original poem, later entitled 'Parting'. The poet's inked corrections I have transcribed in italic.

Breaking Day

He

Dear, I must be gone

While night still shuts the eyes

Of the household spies;
That song announces
~~That lark is shouting of~~ the dawn.

She

No, night's bird and love's

Bids all true lovers rest

While his loud song reproves

The murderous stealth of day.

He

Daylight already flies
~~Day already lies~~
From
~~On that declivitous~~ mountain crest   *to west*

She

That light is from the
~~The newly risen~~ moon   *but not day break*

He

That bird—

She

Let him sing on.

I offer to love's play

My dark declivities.

Only line 3 remains the same as in the early draft on page 6 of the exercise book. The theme is unchanged, and still the debate swings from lark to nightingale, daybreak to moonrise, but everywhere the language has been tightened. Formal stichomythia has been replaced by speech more terse and realistic, culminating in the climactic passage when the man is interrupted, and the subject of the bird dismissed with an arrogant dignity worthy of Cleopatra.

> Let him sing on.
>
> I offer to love's play
>
> My dark declivities.

The best word, like the best wine, has been kept to the last, and not wasted—as was the poet's first intention—in the phrase 'declivitous mountain crest'. The changes in the printed text are few and less important. 'Still' has been dropped from line 2 and instead of 'From mountain crest to west', line 10 reads: 'From mountain crest to crest.'

Though these two poems spring from the one seed, they have grown so far apart that the convolutions of their common root can only be seen by digging in the manuscripts.

VIII

IN MEMORY OF EVA GORE-BOOTH AND CON MARKIEWICZ

I

1. The light of evening, Lissadell,
2. Great windows open to the south,
3. Two girls in silk kimonos, both
4. Beautiful, one a gazelle.
5. But a raving autumn shears
6. Blossom from the summer's wreath;
7. The older is condemned to death,
8. Pardoned, drags out lonely years
9. Conspiring among the ignorant.
10. I know not what the younger dreams—
11. Some vague Utopia—and she seems,
12. When withered old and skeleton-gaunt,
13. An image of such politics.
14. Many a time I think to seek
15. One or the other out and speak
16. Of that old Georgian mansion, mix
17. Pictures of the mind, recall
18. That table and the talk of youth,
19. Two girls in silk kimonos, both
20. Beautiful, one a gazelle.

II

21. Dear shadows, now you know it all,
22. All the folly of a fight
23. With a common wrong or right.
24. The innocent and the beautiful

25. Have no enemy but time;
26. Arise and bid me strike a match
27. And strike another till time catch;
28. Should the conflagration climb,
29. Run till all the sages know.
30. We the great gazebo built,
31. They convicted us of guilt;
32. Bid me strike a match and blow.

••

To be in sympathy with a poet one must understand who and what he is talking about, and this poem cannot make its full impact on the reader who knows nothing of the two women concerned.

Eva Selena Gore-Booth, the third child of Sir Henry Gore-Booth, Bt., was born at Lissadell, Co. Sligo, Ireland, on 22nd May, 1870.

Lissadell is a place of haunting beauty lying near the point of Sligo Bay, between the heather-covered mountains and 'the great waves of the Atlantic':

> The foamless waves are falling soft
> on the sands of Lissadil.

According to the peasants' stories the great cairn on the mountain of Knocknarea, not far away, is the burial-place of the High Queen Maeve.[1]

This fixes Lissadell, geographically, as being in the heart of the 'Yeats' country, and shows Eva to have been five years the poet's junior. Her governess writes:

1882, when I first knew her, is 45 years ago, and I have no notes or diary of any kind. Eva was then, I think, 11 or 12 years old, a very fair fragile-looking child, most unselfish and gentle, with the general look of a Burne-Jones or Botticelli angel. As she was two years younger than Constance (later Markiewicz, her sister), and always so delicate, she had been, I think, rather in the background and a little lonely mentally,

---

[1] Esther Roper, introduction to *Poems of Eva Gore-Booth*, 1929, p. 5.

but music was a great joy to her. The symbolic side of religion had just then a great charm for her, and always of course the mystical side of everything appealed most. . . . Though her sight was always bad, she was an absolutely fearless rider. . . .[1]

This last quality Yeats particularly admired in the elder sister. He mentions Constance's riding to harriers in the poem 'Easter 1916', and again in that 'On a Political Prisoner', written when she was in Holloway gaol:

> When long ago I saw her ride
> Under Ben Bulben to the meet,
> The beauty of her country-side
> With all youth's lonely wildness stirred,
> She seemed to have grown clean and sweet
> Like any rock-bred, sea-borne bird:

A photograph of the sisters in their youth shows both to have been beautiful, but does not prepare one for the astonishing loveliness of the elder, whose full-length portrait in the Dublin Municipal Gallery hangs opposite that of Maud Gonne. In the exquisite moulding of the ice-cold face and the tall, imperious figure, she seems no less suited to the role of a latter-day Helen than her more famous contemporary.

Writing to Eva in 1916, Yeats says: 'Your sister and yourself, two beautiful figures among the great trees of Lissadell, are among the dear memories of my youth.'[2] In 1897, when she decided to publish her first book of poems, he wrote to her: 'I think it is full of poetic feeling and has great promise'.[3] Like him she was absorbed in Irish history and mythology. Her book *Unseen Kings*, published in 1904, included a play on the death of Cuchulain.

Although both sisters were brought up in the aristocratic environment and traditions, which Yeats so reverenced, and although both were presented at court, an intense awareness of the sufferings of the poor—inherited from a kindly father—drew them away from the attractions of high society. By 1897 Eva was in Manchester, working for the Women's Suffrage Movement and the struggling trades unions. She spoke well on political and economic subjects and became a practised public speaker.

---

[1] Esther Roper, introduction to *Poems of Eva Gore-Booth*, 1929, p. 6.
[2] Ibid., p. 7.   [3] Ibid., p. 9.

Constance, who had a considerable talent for painting, in 1900 met and married a fellow artist, Count Casimir Markiewicz. After living for some time in Russia, they moved to Dublin, where their home became a noted gathering place for writers, painters, politicians, and trade unionists. With what Esther Roper describes as 'radiant energy'[1] Constance threw herself into social work of all kinds. In 1909 she organized the Irish Scout Movement, and at all times helped the poor in the slums of Dublin.

From 1913 she had identified herself with the Trade Union movement, whose leader was James Connolly. For six months (at the time of the great strike there) she had, almost single-handed, run a canteen for the feeding of the starving children—collecting the money, buying and cooking the food herself. . . . She was an honorary official of the Transport Workers' Union and an officer in their Citizen Army. (Later she was in the first Republican Cabinet as Minister for Labour, and did very able work.)[2]

She also wrote rebel, propagandist plays, such as *Blood Money*, *The Invincible Mother*, and *Broken Dreams*: in some she acted, and her experience of the stage was later to stand her in good stead when in disguise and on the run from the police.

In the Easter rebellion of 1916 she was Second in Command of the Citizen Army Force in Stephen's Green. With the other leaders she was court-martialled and sentenced to death: seventeen were executed, and the remainder, including Madame (as Constance was known in Dublin), though reprieved, were sent to convict prisons. Here the close bond of sympathy between the sisters was a source of comfort and strength to them both. In a letter of July 1926, Con wrote:

When I was in Aylesbury (prison) we agreed to try to get in touch a few minutes every day, and I used to sit at about six o'clock and think of her and concentrate and try and leave my mind a blank, a sort of dark, still pool, and I got to her, and once I told her how she sat in a window, and I seemed to know what she was thinking.[3]

Eva died in 1926, Constance in 1927, and in September[4] of that year Yeats began a poem to their memory. The manuscript is on

[1] Introduction to *Prison Letters of Countess Markievicz*, 1934, p. 4.
[2] Introduction to *Poems of Eva Gore-Booth*, 1929, p. 23.   [3] Ibid., p. 39.
[4] Not October, as Ellmann states in *The Identity of Yeats*, 1954, p. 291.

three loose-leaf sheets, and there is a single typescript. F. 1r of the manuscript contains a rough draft of the poem 'From the "Antigone" ', which appears finally as number XI of 'A Woman Young and Old'. The fact that these are respectively the first and last poems in *The Winding Stair and Other Poems*, although presumably written at approximately the same time, is an interesting commentary on the care with which Yeats arranged his work for publication.

The draft working of 'In Memory of Eva Gore-Booth and Con Markiewicz', part I, occurs on F. 1v and F. 2r of the manuscript, which in the original loose-leaf notebook would have faced each other. As usual, Yeats began on the right, on F. 2r:

> A Georgian house under a hill
>
> (   ) the glittering subject & my own
>
> A (   ) summer evening of youth
>
> A table in the sunlight, youth

This opening he improves on the left-hand page:

> Sunlight upon sea & hill
>
> A table spread,
>
> A table & window to the south
>
> The light of evening, Lissadell
> A w
> Windows opening to the south

Returning to the right-hand page he changes the second line:

> Great windows open to the south

and continues:

> Two girls in silk kimonos, both
>
> Both beautiful, one a gazelle
>
> exquisite & sensitive —
>
> Contagion of the popular breath

On the left-hand page his bitter disillusionment gets the better of him:

~~But Ireland is a hag & seems~~

~~What she touches with her breath~~

Muzzling his anger, and resisting the temptation to digress, he returns—on the right—more closely to the central theme:

~~The summer foliage disappears~~

~~Under the October breath~~

But the spring to summer wears

That brings round October breath

There follows a line in which I can only decipher the one word, 'blunders'. He is thinking, I believe, of the blunders of Easter 1916. On the left he attempts to make a transition from the 'glorious summer' to 'the winter of their discontent'.

~~What distinguished calm endures~~

~~How could she it be they survive~~

~~But where~~
        happiness
How can ~~loveliness~~ survive

Abandoning all rhetorical questions, he begins again—on the right —with a stark and telling statement:

       The ~~older~~ is
stronger| *~~One is~~ condemned to death*
      Pardoned but
    ~~But pardoned & elects to live~~ *~~drags out long years~~*

Conspiring among the ignorant

On the left-hand page he tightens up line 8:

pardoned drags out weary years

On the right he now calls to mind his memories of Eva:

~~The younger The gentler~~ *~~life & labour seem~~*

~~All the younger's labour seems~~ The younger ~~enduring~~ dream
                   makes things seem
~~Abstract humanitarian dream.~~ The abstraction of a dream

Her body grown skeleton gaunt,

A ~~fitting~~ symbol ~~of it all~~ of her politics

Many a time I think to seek

One or the other out & speak
                mansion
Of that ~~old~~ Georgian ~~house &~~ mix
  Her
~~Their~~ memories & my memories

~~Of of the~~

~~sunlight (———)~~   ~~conversation of our youth~~

~~Memories of sea & hill~~   ~~memory with memory until~~
  That
~~Of this conversation of our youth~~ ~~That table there, the talk of youth~~

~~Two girls in silk kimonos both~~

~~Beautiful one a gazelle.~~

Triumphantly, on the left-hand page, he compresses his scattered thoughts into four lines that half-echo the poem's opening:

Pictures of the mind recall

That table & the talk of youth

Two girls in silk kimonos, both

Beautiful, one a gazelle.

I say half-echo, because 'That table' is not mentioned before, in the final version, but only in such crossed-out lines as:

~~A table in the sunlight, youth~~

After the sharply visual memory picture of part I, which, as it were, sets the scene, in part II Yeats closes the gap still further, and directly addresses the two girls. Only now they are girls no longer, but 'Dear shadows'. The poem's two parts represent past and present. The manuscript of part II is written on F. 2v and F. 3r, which in Yeats's notebook would have faced each other. He begins uncertainly on the right:

~~No~~

~~You be~~   *Learn dear shadows in the grave*

~~(————) now beyond the grave~~
                  All the folly of a fight
~~That such as ye should never fight~~
                  wrong
With a common ~~rong~~ or right

That innocence & beauty have

No enemy but time & love
          arise & bid me
~~Dear ghosts return~~ *& strike a match*
          strike
And ~~yet~~ another till time catch

~~And (————————)~~

~~A bellow~~

~~Some great bellows to a fyre~~
                great
Some ~~(————)~~ *bellows to a fire*
      For
~~Have not a~~ *widow Nature still*
      Has
~~All~~ *those cradles left to fill*

And works of intellectual fire
          and we that toil
Account ~~(————————)~~ *are few*

This very rough draft has been crossed out with diagonal lines.
Before exploring what the passage means, I give a second version
of the last five lines, written to the right of the draft already
quoted:

> *And when the final embers gone*
>
> *Bid me let the sages know*
>
> *I the great gazebo built*
>
> *They brought home to me the guilt*
>
> *Bid me strike a match & blow.*

Under this is written the date, 'Sept. 21'.

The introductory lines of the draft do not differ much from the finished text. They are followed, however, by a chiasmus which the poet was later to reduce to simpler terms:

That innocence & beauty have

No enemy but time & love

Time is the enemy of beauty and love the enemy of innocence. 'Love' is cut out of the poem because it is irrelevant, and the reader's attention must be focused on time, which in this context becomes the enemy of both beauty and innocence. Time is the great enemy: it has wrecked and finally killed the

Two girls in silk kimonos, both

Beautiful, one a gazelle.

In the midst of his tragic reflections Yeats finds his imagination caught in a heroic and apocalyptic vision. The two girls shall be revenged on their enemy. Saul suggests that 'We the great gazebo built' means 'We provided the lofty, wide outlook'; and on one level I believe Yeats means the gazebo to represent his early vision, more romantic than realistic, of a resurgent Ireland. From the detachment of their ivory tower, he and such of his friends as the Gore-Booth sisters, had imagined their countrymen casting off the yoke of England, fired by the spirits of Cuchulain and the ancient heroes. The gazebo may also be a metaphor for 'time' in line 27 (was it perhaps unconsciously suggested by 'folly' in line 22?). Time-present (from which one can gaze on time-past and time-future) is a structure they have built themselves. If they could build it, they can destroy it: reason is swept aside by imagination. The 'Dear Shadows' have only to bid him take a match, but no voices answer from the grave and the visionary moment passes—in the first draft:

Nature still

Has

~~*All*~~ *those cradles left to fill*

In the second draft, however, the visionary moment is extended. He no longer admits that the conflagration is an impossible daydream, and even looks beyond it.

And when the final embers gone

Bid me let the sages know

When time has been destroyed and the past undone, he is to inform the sages, who already exist outside time. These sages must be religious figures, like the 'sages standing in God's holy fire', or the sage who is Christ and appears in one of the drafts of 'Coole Park 1929'. Here they seem to symbolize Religion (unspecified, of course), which brought home to the poet some guilt resultant on building the gazebo. This at first he claims as his own work, and if on a general level the gazebo represents his early vision and time/history, on the particular level it is a metaphor for the history of Easter 1916. Looking back on the rebellion Yeats, I think, was apt to confuse his dreams of personal heroism with the real and tragic heroism of so many of his friends. He liked to think of himself as a rebel—

> Did that play of mine send out
> Certain men the English shot?—

and was eager to assume a share in the guilt, because with it went a share of the glory, although strictly he was entitled to neither. In this first draft of the poem he distorts its perspective, by shifting the ultimate emphasis from the two sisters to himself:

I the great gazebo built

They brought home to me the guilt

Bid me strike a match & blow.

This is not altered in the rough draft on the left-hand page of the manuscript:

>   *they*
> *Dead, ~~you~~ know what living meant*
>
> *All the folly of a fight*
>
> *With a common wrong or right*
>
> *The beautiful & innocent*

> *Have no enemy but time*
>
> *Dear shadows bid me strike a match*
>
> *Dead you know what*
>
> *Should the conflagration climb*
>
> *Bid me let etc*

He has here changed his opening apostrophe, and reversed the adjectives 'innocent & beautiful' to make the rhyme: here, too, is the first appearance of 'Should the conflagration climb'.

Although in the *Variorum* this poem is dated October 1927, the typescript, which is still some way from the finished text, is dated 'Seville, Nov. 1927'. It reads:

I

> A Georgian house under a hill
>
> Great windows open to the south,
>
> Two girls in silk kimonos, both
>
> Beautiful, one a gazelle.
>
> But a raving Autumn shears
>
> Blossom from the summer's wreath;
>
> The older is condemned to death,
>
> Pardoned, drags out lonely years
>
> Conspiring among the ignorant.
>
> The younger's dream makes all things seem
>
> The abstraction of a dream
>
> Her body grows skeleton-gaunt
>
> The symbol of her politics.
>
> Many a time I think to seek

One or the other out and speak

Of that old Georgian mansion, mix

Pictures of the mind, recall

That table and the talk of youth,

Two girls in silk kimonos, both

Beautiful, one a gazelle.

II

Dear shadows, now you know it all,

All the folly of a fight

With a common wrong or right.

The beautiful and innocent

Have no enemy but time;

Dear shadows bid me strike a match

And strike another till time catch;

Should the conflagration climb,

Run till all the sages know.

We the great gazebo built,

They brought home to me the guilt;

Bid me strike a match and blow.

Here, the most significant improvement is in part II. The colloquial beginning is more vigorous:

Dear shadows, now you know it all,

All the folly of a fight

With a common wrong or right.

The subjective 'I' has vanished from the poem's close: 'We' takes its place, as, linking himself with his subject, Yeats corrects the faulty perspective.

The final changes are more minor but two are worthy of mention. 'A Georgian house under a hill' is replaced by the more specific and evocative line, which also appeared in the manuscript drafts: 'The light of evening, Lissadell,'. Lines 10–13, which in the typescript were stiff and unrhythmical, are given a new colloquial freedom:

> I know not what the younger dreams—
> Some vague Utopia—and she seems,
> When withered old and skeleton-gaunt,
> An image of such politics.

The finished poem moves with a disarming conversational fluency to its metaphysical conclusion. Its language and cadences are those of natural speech, but its apparent artlessness is a triumph of the 'maker's' art.

IX

COOLE PARK, 1929

1. I meditate upon a swallow's flight,
2. Upon an aged woman and her house,
3. A sycamore and lime-tree lost in night
4. Although that western cloud is luminous,
5. Great works constructed there in nature's spite
6. For scholars and for poets after us,
7. Thoughts long knitted into a single thought,
8. A dance-like glory that those walls begot.

9. There Hyde before he had beaten into prose
10. That noble blade the Muses buckled on,
11. There one that ruffled in a manly pose
12. For all his timid heart, there that slow man,
13. That meditative man, John Synge, and those
14. Impetuous men, Shawe-Taylor and Hugh Lane,
15. Found pride established in humility,
16. A scene well set and excellent company.

17. They came like swallows and like swallows went,
18. And yet a woman's powerful character
19. Could keep a swallow to its first intent;
20. And half a dozen in formation there,
21. That seemed to whirl upon a compass-point,
22. Found certainty upon the dreaming air,
23. The intellectual sweetness of those lines
24. That cut through time or cross it withershins.

25. Here, traveller, scholar, poet, take your stand
26. When all those rooms and passages are gone,

27. When nettles wave upon a shapeless mound
28. And saplings root among the broken stone,
29. And dedicate—eyes bent upon the ground,
30. Back turned upon the brightness of the sun
31. And all the sensuality of the shade—
32. A moment's memory to that laurelled head.

YEATS's friendship with Lady Gregory had begun as far back as 1896, when he stayed for the first time at Coole, the Gregorys' family home. It remained unbroken until her death in May 1932. During the many summers spent under her roof Yeats did much of his writing, for the noble house with its seven woods had a stronger hold on his affections and his imagination than any home of his own, with the exception of Thoor Ballylee. The remarkable mistress of this house first became acquainted with it when, as Augusta Persse and the twelfth of sixteen children, she was invited by Sir William Gregory to browse in its fine library. Unlike her crack-shot, hard-riding brothers, she was passionately interested in books: and so delighted Sir William, an ex-Governor of Ceylon, with her company, that despite the thirty-five years difference in their ages, he made her his wife. At his side she was introduced to both influential and intellectual society, until in 1892 he died, leaving her mistress of Coole.

It was to fill this gap in her life that she first set about learning Irish and collecting folk-lore. In this, as later in the writing of plays for the Abbey Theatre, she worked with Yeats. Her researches had by then marvellously attuned her ear to the syntax and inflexions of peasant speech. In addition to the literary gift that produced in *The Rising of the Moon* and *Devorgilla* comedy and tragedy, she had great gifts of character. Though her latter

years were darkened by the tragic death on active service of her
adored son Robert, she put her courage, humanity and perseverance
to splendid use in the service of the Abbey Theatre, and in the
battle for possession of the Lane pictures.

Because the poet's sombre prophecy of Coole has been fulfilled—

> nettles wave upon a shapeless mound
> And saplings root among the broken stone,

we must go to Joseph Hone,[1] his first biographer, for a description
of the house and park as Yeats would have known them:

The unpretentious gates of Coole open on an avenue of great trees,
their leafy embracing branches a tunnel of twilight on the sunniest day.
The avenue curves through wood and fields to a modest white-fronted
house, rather like a large Italian farm-house, which looks across a wide
sloping field to a great wood. On the left of the house are walled
pleasure-grounds, where may still be seen the catalpa tree under which
Yeats and George Moore quarrelled over their play, *Diarmuid and
Grania*, also a giant copper beech, its trunk carved over with initials of
many famous men: W. B. Y., A.E., G. B. S., Ian H. (Ian Hamilton),
J. M. S. (Synge), A. J. (Augustus John), J. M. (Masefield). More woods
spread out behind the house, the paths lost; at the confines of the
demesne, in a landscape of mysterious and desolate beauty, as though
one were at the world's end, lies a grey lake with wild swans. . . .

> The trees are in their autumn beauty,
> The woodland paths are dry,
> Under the October twilight the water
> Mirrors a still sky;
> Upon the brimming water among the stones
> Are nine-and-fifty swans.

At Coole Yeats found a life of order and of labour where all outward
things were the signatures of an inward life. In his childhood, at his
grandfather's, he had learned to love an elaborate house, a garden and
park, and those grey country houses of Sligo—Lissadell, Hazelwood
and the more rarely seen towers of Markree—had always called to his
mind a life set amid natural beauty and the activities of servants and
labourers, who seemed themselves natural, as birds and trees are
natural. Many generations, and no uncultured generation, had left
images of their service in the outlines of wood and fields at Coole, in
sculpture and pictures, in furniture, in a fine library with editions of the
classics and books on plants and agriculture. Her Galway home was
Lady Gregory's passion. . . .

[1] *W. B. Yeats, 1865–1939*, 1942, pp. 138–40.

A letter written by Sir Ian Hamilton in 1908 gives a lively picture of the house, and the poet at work:

"Yeats and I were the only guests in the big house. Yeats unfortunately for my enjoyment was in the throes of composition and was being thoroughly spoilt. No one can ever have heard anyone play up to him like Lady Gregory. His bedroom was halfway down a passage on the first floor at the end of which was my room. All along the passage for some distance on either side of Yeats's door were laid thick rugs to prevent the slightest sound reaching the holy of holies—Yeats's bed. Down the passage every now and then would tiptoe a maid with a tray bearing (they told me) beef tea or arrowroot, though once I declare I distinctly smelt eggs and bacon. All suggestions that I could cheer him up a good deal if I went into his room and had a chat were met with horror. What I said about his groans and grumbles is hardly correct for they only came to me by hearsay through Lady Gregory and the servants. Actually I never once set eyes upon the aristocratic features of my friend Yeats on that occasion."

The poem to which Sir Ian refers was probably either 'Galway Races' or the lines—Yeats's first on a political occasion since Parnell's death—on the refusal of the Government to appoint Hugh Lane curator of the Dublin National Museum.[1]

This then is the background to the poem 'Coole Park, 1929'. The drafts are to be found on thirty-eight pages of Manuscript Book B, which I have numbered 1–38, in their order of composition, although this is not the order in which they occur in the book. First mention of the poem is the following 'prose sketch' on page 1:

Poem on Coole to go with Lady G.'s

Cuala essays

Prose sketch

~~To this house~~   *Describe Lady G.*
Describe house in first stanza. Here Synge came,

Hugh Lane, Shaw Taylor, many names. I too in my timid

youth, coming & going like the migratory birds.

Then address the swallows flitting in their dream like circles

[1] J. M. Hone, *W. B. Yeats, 1865–1939*, 1942, p. 225.

> ~~all the~~ most
> speak of the rarity of the circumstances, that bring together
>
> such concords of men. ~~each man more than himself~~
>
> ~~through whom an unknown life speaks. a circle ever returning~~
>
> ~~into itself, &c.~~

The poem proper begins with rough jottings on pages 2 and 3:
these are gathered together on page 4:

> ~~And for the~~
> But for the generations after us
>   sing
> I ~~praise~~ miraculous intricacies
>
> ~~Old amities~~
>
> ~~Or amities~~
>
> Amities of skill, amities of kind thought
>
> A dance like glory that these walls begot
>
> I sing what seemed natural amities
>   passion
> Of ancient ~~passions~~ & intricate thought—
>
> A dance like glory that these walls begot
>
>
> I sing miraculous intricacies
>
> ~~Old amities of skill, amities of thought~~
>
> ~~Made in friendship, & in skill~~
>
> ~~Friendship, imagination, or skillful skill~~
>
> ~~Skill & imagination, friendly thought~~
>
> ~~Imagination daring friendly thought~~
>
> Of new thoughts knitted to a common thought
>
> A dance like glory that these walls begot

These two sketches for a stanza have a line drawn through them,
and at the foot of the page Yeats drafts a rough rhyme-plan:

J. Synge	*Hyde*	*Lane*		
man		~~man~~		
~~Lane~~		*Synge*	*A*	A
imagining		man	~~BC~~	1
Lane		imagining	~~B~~	B
wing		Lane	~~BD~~	2
countenance		( )		C
		( )		
		( )		3

On page 5 he gives stanza I a definite shape, though not its final
one:

> I praise for pleasure an intricate house
>   for
> ~~I praise my heart's sake ancient house~~
>   set about the wood's
> ~~About about the wood the wood's intricacies,~~
>   among
> ~~Shadowed by foliage or lake luminous~~
>
> ~~Foot worn, wheel worn or wing beaten ways~~
>
> *   Among the foliage shadowed, a lake luminous
>   or old
> *   Old foot worn, wheel worn, wing worn ways
>   that come
> ~~But~~ for the generations after us
>   strange
> I (   ) praise (   ) amities
>
> Of new thoughts knitted to a common thought
>
> A dance like glory that the walls begot

Crossing out the last four lines, he rewrites the stanza improving
lines 1, 2, 5, 6, and 7:

> I praise for pleasure that intricate house
>
> Set among the wood's intricacies
>
> Among the foliage shadowed, a lake luminous
>
> Old foot worn, wheel worn, or old wing worn ways

       * Inserted from the top of the page.

to
But ~~for~~ *the generations after us*

Commend unnatural, deep amities
                    knitted into
~~All~~ *thoughts long (   ) a single thought*

A dance like glory that those walls begot.

Below this, he tentatively revises lines 7 and 3:

of ~~Thoughts knitted into a single thought~~

And overhead the cloudy, luminous

   In this state for the moment he leaves stanza I, although ultimately only the concluding couplet was to survive. There is a firm
enough rhetorical framework to this stanza, but lines 1 and 6, in
particular, are weak, and the reader is unprepared for the 'dance
like glory'. Nor, as yet, is there more than an oblique allusion
('old wing worn ways') to the swallows that were eventually to
begin the poem, and to provide its central image.
   Yeats now turns his attention to stanza II, and on pages 6 and
7 scribbles down such lines and fragments of lines as:

Here Hyde . . .

Those daring men Shaw Taylor and Hugh Lane . . .

Douglas Hyde, like Hugh Lane, was the son of an Irish country
rector. Before going to Trinity College, Dublin, where he won
numerous prizes, Hyde learnt Irish orally from the natives of
Roscommon, and recorded a wealth of folk-lore and poetry. Himself a gifted poet, playwright, and literary historian, he was the
first president of the Gaelic League, and one of the most ener-
getic pioneers of the Irish Renascence. His resolute avoidance of
political controversy forced him to resign his presidency of the
Gaelic League in 1915, but he was nominated for a seat in the
Senate in 1925: and in 1937, when all parties were searching for
a candidate 'above and apart from politics', he was invited by
unanimous request to become the first President of Eire.
   In his essay on John Shawe-Taylor in *The Cutting of an Agate*,
Yeats wrote that he was 'a good soldier and a good shot and a good

rider to hounds'. Immaculate in hunting pink, he stares out of
Orpen's fine romantic portrait in the Municipal Gallery. Like
Robert Gregory, he was killed in the First World War, and in his
youth had seemed to the poet an ideal of cultured and chivalrous
nobility:

> Soldier, scholar, horseman, he,
> As 'twere all life's epitome.

Hugh Lane, Lady Gregory's nephew, having come to London
as a young man to learn the techniques of picture-dealing, had
there set up on his own at the age of twenty-three. So expert
became his knowledge and so sure his judgement, that he soon
made a fortune. At Coole in 1900 he first met Yeats, and determined to launch a movement in Irish art parallel to the Irish
literary revival. He commissioned portraits, arranged exhibitions,
helped to found the Municipal Gallery, and eventually offered a
substantial collection of French Impressionist paintings to the
Dublin Corporation on condition that they provided a permanent
gallery. Their refusal to do this precipitated a bitter controversy
in which Yeats took a lively part, writing such poems as 'September
1913' and 'Paudeen'. Lane then bequeathed them to the English
National Gallery, but in a codicil to his will, which because of his
early death at the sinking of the *Lusitania* was never witnessed, he
restored them to the Harcourt Street Collection. Until a just
compromise was effected in 1960, the paintings remained in London; and the Dublin Municipal Gallery, with a gesture of which
Yeats would have approved, kept one room empty in silent, though
eloquent, protest.

As stanza II takes shape on page 8, however, it is not these
visitors to Coole who take pride of place, but the poet himself:

> *Here one long tossed by every wind that blows*
>
> *A weather cock, shuttle cock, comedian comeleon*
>
> *Here beaten on by every wind that blows*
>
> *Here one a straw on every wind that blows*
> *A weather comeleon cock or comelean*
> *A weather cock shuttle cock comelean comeleon*

>   ~~And~~   *folly that* *Youth*
> *Adding to the ~~follies~~ that*   *shows*
>   *here that quiet*
> *Hatred and terror : ~~that slow thinking~~ man*
>
> *That meditative man John Synge ; and those*
>   ~~Unfortunate~~
> ~~Bold hearted~~ *men Shaw-Taylor & Hugh Lane*
>
> *Found pride established in humility*
>
> *A scene well set & excellent company.*
>
> ~~Here one, fresh from every wind that blows~~
>
> ~~A weather cock shuttle cock comelean,~~
>
> ~~Here fresh from~~
>
>   *light*
> *Here a straw on every wind that blows*
>
> *Here I beaten by every wind that blows*
>
> *The character of my own mind unknown*
>   *youth's*
> *But hiding under ~~a~~ embittered pose*
>
> *That ignorance ; here a slow thinking man*
>
> *A meditative man John Synge & those*
>
> *Most daring men Shaw Taylor & Hugh Lane etc*
>
> *Found pride established in humility*
>
> *A scene well set & excellent company.*

Before proceeding to a less subjective version of this stanza, Yeats crossed these drafts out with diagonal lines. 'Weather cock, shuttle cock, cameleon' he has already wisely abandoned: the juxtaposition of cock and chameleon (especially when mis-spelt) is not a happy one. One chapter in *The Trembling of the Veil* is entitled 'Hodos Chameliontos', which he explains: 'I was lost in that region a cabbalistic manuscript shown me by MacGregor Mathers, had warned me of; astray upon the Path of the Chameleon, upon Hodos Chameliontos.'[1] I think it also possible that Yeats had in mind Keats's remarks about 'The chameleon poet', who loses all personal identity, so closely does he identify himself with his changing subject-matter. Yeats can never be said to lose his identity, even when he wears the mask, but he admits to being 'a light straw on every wind that blows'. When he recasts the stanza II on page 9, Douglas Hyde has taken his place at the head of the procession, but still Yeats refers to himself in the first person:

> ~~Here Hyde, (   ) mechanical (   ) begun~~
>   ~~sword scarce beaten~~
> ~~His The muses' sword scarce beaten into prose~~

> Here ~~Douglas~~ Hyde, before he had beaten into prose
>   That noble the muses buckled
> ~~The sword~~ blade ~~that the muses~~ had ~~buckled~~ on

> Here I covering with youth's embittered pose
>   Hatred & terror
> ~~Great ignorance~~; here that slow thinking man
>   here
> That meditative man John Synge, ~~&~~ those

> Here I, covering with a boy's confident pose

> Hatred & terror

> Here I, hiding under an embittered pose

> A boy's timidity; here that slow man

> That meditative man John Synge & those

> Impetuous men &c.

Here, for the moment, he leaves this stanza. Its adjectives in particular he has improved: 'slow-thinking', which is uncomplimentary, to 'slow': 'bold hearted', 'unfortunate', and 'most daring' to 'impetuous'.

 Following the plan of his initial prose sketch, he begins stanza III, on page 10, with a direct address to the swallows:

[1] W. B. Yeats, *Autobiographies*, 1955, p. 270.

O swallow

O dusky tears

O blackness with a sudden gleam of white

O swallow

O world hovering swallow that can fill

With such deft circles the approach of night
    With A   *or*
the waltz or old Sir Roger of quadrill

Who taught the mathematics of their flight?

Who taught the sweetness of a common will?
    What
What frenzy or what learning makes you seem

A motion with the certainty of a dream—

                or

Nor taught

Who taught –

Who learn or taught—what learning dare attempt
    (   )
Nor dared to (   ) no scholar to attempt

                or

Who taught a turning & returning, that can seem

Drawn with the decorum of a dream

The last eight lines have been crossed out with a diagonal line. The swallows at this stage are more realistic than symbolic. As they weave gracefully before him in a pattern which seems to the poet no less ordered than the old, eighteenth-century dances, he asks them his rhetorical questions: who taught them their precision and their skill? He does not give the answer, but it can only be God.

On page 11 he plots a rhyme scheme for stanza III ('white,

 port

skill, night, drille, flight, will, seem, dream') and on page 12 proceeds to a full draft of the poem so far:

Coole House

I

       ears   ancient
   for living ~~eyes~~ that ancient house
I praise ~~for pleasure that intricate~~ house

Set among the woods' intricacies

Among the foliage shadowed a lake luminous

Old foot worn, wheel worn, or old wing worn ways

But to the generations after us ~~commend~~

Commend unnatural deep, amities

Thoughts long knitted into a single thought   stet

A dance like glory that those walls begot

II

Here Hyde before he had beaten into prose

That noble blade the Muses buckled on;
    under an embittered pose
Here I, ~~covering with a boy's confident pose~~
   A boy's timidity
~~Hatred & terror~~; here that slow ~~thinking~~ man
                 and
That meditative man John Synge; ~~here~~ those
   Impetuous
~~Most daring~~ men Shaw Taylor & Hugh Lane

Found pride established in humility,

A scene well set & excellent company

III

~~O sooty black & sudden of white~~

~~O trivial (   ) swallows that can fill~~

~~With such deft circles the approach of night~~

~~A~~ *Waltz, or old Sir Roger or quadrille*

Who taught the mathematics of their flight?
     Or who
Who taught the sweetness of a common will?
— — — —

~~What was your academy that seems~~

~~Lost in the~~

~~But the intricate certainty of a dream.~~

Stanza III has been crossed out, and below it written a possible alteration for line 22, and the final form of line 11:

transfiguring will?

Here one that ruffled with a manly pose

Facing this draft, on page 13 are corrections to stanzas I and III:

~~Among the living woods' intricacies~~

Among the nests, under the luminous

Storm tormented clouds connaught skies
          under
~~And overhead the lofty luminous~~

Cloud encumbered stormy western skies
               scholars that come
But to the ~~generations after us~~

Commend miraculous consanguinities
          ~~long~~
Thought knitted into a single thought
                              they
Who taught those travelled swallows that fill

With that great dancing the approach of night
     Or what academy of
~~Who taught intricacies of~~ *black & white*

A labyrinthe of sudden lines that seem

Driven into the decorum of a dream

The changes are interesting. The reference to 'nests' brings the birds into greater prominence: it is now their element—the skies— that is luminous rather than the lake. 'Generations' has been crossed out, in favour of the more specific 'scholars'. 'Miraculous consanguinities' is both a stronger and more evocative phrase than 'unnatural deep amities'.

This thought seems to have led him into the drafts of a puzzling version of stanza IV on page 14:

IV

Remembering those birds that shared their blood

"Where two or three are gathered" said the sage

And flung a pastime to the multitude.[1]

The ~~pillar's marble~~ marble portico, the preacher's rage,

The merry organ & the pilgrim's rood,

Protecting with this cloudy heritage

Those great characters of the living word

The bodies of a dancer & a bird.

If I could find some fitting few he said

Some two or three together & the sage   bestowed

Flung out a pastime to the multitude[1]   road

The marble portico, the preacher's rage

The martyr's fagot & the pilgrim's rood

Protecting etc.

"Where two or three are gathered"—He bestowed,

The marble portico, the preacher's rage

[1] 'pastime' is a tentative reading.

That abstract mystery of the pilgrim's ~~road rage~~

The martyr's fagot on the mu

The last ten lines have been crossed out with a diagonal line. Yeats makes a fresh attempt on page 15:

"Where two or three are gathered—" he bestowed

That blinding temper of the middle age

That abstract passion of the pilgrim's rood

The martyr's faggot & the preacher's rage

All that phantasy of the multitude.

Beneath these five lines in ink he wrote, raggedly, in pencil:

~~*"Where*~~

~~*"Something is but of that" the eleven said*~~

~~*A*~~

~~*"Where two or three"*~~ ~~*& (   ) the word*~~
                        ~~*spoke to them*~~ *the word*
~~*"Where two or three are gathered there am I,*~~
                                                    that
"Where two or three are gathered" ~~*Jesus said*~~ *said* ~~*the*~~ *sage*
                                              the
Who promised nothing to ~~*that*~~ *multitude*

~~*The prelate's will, the preacher's rage*~~

His pencil wanders on for a further eleven half-lines, many of which are illegible. The biblical quotation is from Matthew xviii. 20: 'Where two or three are gathered together in my name, there am I in the midst of them.' This is not so violent a switch of direction as at first appears, since 'God' was the answer to the poet's earlier rhetorical question: 'Who taught the sweetness of a common will?' Christ's words have, I believe, been taken from their context to provide a link between the idea of the swallows' 'miraculous consanguinity', and the 'deep amities' existing between Lady Gregory's friends. But if God is at the centre of one circle, and Lady Gregory at the centre of the other, the equation becomes ridiculous. The catalogued paraphernalia of Christianity is as utterly foreign to a poem on Coole, as the introduction of Christ himself: and Yeats very wisely abandons the whole stanza. Instead, he turns to a consideration of Lady Gregory and her house. Pages 16–29 contain scattered and random jottings for stanzas III and IV, such as 'A woman here had such great character' and the couplet (on page 22):

> *That famous work completed—none could say*
>
> *Whether her will or ours had won the day.*

'That famous work' I take to be the foundation of the Abbey Theatre. The drafts of stanza IV, with its ominous prophecy of the future of Coole, culminate in that on page 30:

> *Here student, unknown traveller take your stand*
>
> *~~Whenever~~*
>
> *When these strong ash saplings root among the stones*
>
> *~~& briar & nettle~~ And briar & nettle's edge*
>
> *~~& briar & nettle~~*
>
> *And ~~plots of briar~~ shade a shapeless mound*
>   *~~consecrate~~*
> *~~And dedicate eyes fixed upon~~*
>
> *The resurrection of the foliage round*
>   *~~That when~~*   *~~handy work is gone~~*
> *That when the noblest handy work is gone*
>
> *Cast the ostentation of a shade*
>
> *A ~~moment's~~ memory to this laurelled head*
>
>   *And fix your eyes upon*
> *~~Now ever upon the spring~~ or summer sun*
>
> *The resurrection of the foliage round*
>   *~~And~~ Here Here*   *~~the~~*
> *Here dedicate, ~~here~~ amid fallen stone*

Here
~~Here~~ *amid the ostentation of the shade*

A moment's memory to the laurelled head

Amid that indistinguishable shade

A moment's memory

At this point he would seem to have gone back to the troublesome stanza III, and page 31 reads:

We came like swallows & like swallows went

~~The (   ) a swallow will~~

~~Some in weaving flight swallow will~~
          had
A woman there such great character

~~A score~~ *That half a score of swallows in*

~~And half a score like well content~~

~~To measure out a circle in the air~~

~~To cut such lines & such character~~

~~To draw a~~

To

To wheel & cut a figure in the air

As though it turned upon a compas point

She had such intellect & character

These lines he crossed out with a diagonal line, and continued below with the opening of stanza I:

I praise for living ears an ancient house
           her
The woman of that house, ~~&~~ *western skies*

Stormy cloudy encumbered, luminous

This shows no advance on the preceding drafts, and on page 32 he returns to stanza III:

> We came like swallows & like swallows went
>   ~~And yet~~   or so stayed circling
> Yet half a score ~~it may be circled~~ there
>   compass
> And though they wheeled upon a ~~compas~~ point
> (   ) a dance or a (   )
> ~~And cut so quaint a measure~~ in the air
>   stayed in
> And never had they ~~changed~~ their intent
>
> But for that woman's powerful character
>   And   never had that magic circle gone
> ~~Nor would that work of magic have been done~~
>
> Against the repetitions of the sun

Slowly he organizes his material and brings together the images of men and swallows. The references to magic are not, I think, intended to be understood literally, for Lady Gregory had little or nothing to do with Yeats's researches into the occult. 'Magic circle' I take to mean 'miraculous consanguinities' as reflected in the company's bond of fellowship that time and again brought them together.

On page 33 the poem advances to its first full draft:

> I
>
>   an
> I praise for living ears ~~that~~ ancient house,
>
> Intricate in the woods' intricacies,
>   A woman in that house but
> ~~The A windy water's edge, the luminous,~~
>
> Tormented, cloud encumbered connaught skies;
>
> But for the scholars that come after us
>   unnatural
> Commend ~~miraculous~~ consanguinities,
>
> Thoughts knitted into a single thought,
>
> A dance like glory that those walls begot

~~II~~ 2

Here Hyde before he had beaten into prose

That noble blade the muses buckled on;

Here one that ruffled in a manly pose

For all his timid heart; here that slow man

That meditative man John Synge & those

Impetuous men Shaw Taylor & Hugh Lane

Found pride established in humility

A scene well set & excellent company.

III

*   They*
~~We~~ *came like swallows & like swallows went;*

Yet half a score or so stayed circling ~~there~~ here

As though they wheeled upon a compass point
~~(   )~~   (   )
~~(   ) geometricians of the air~~

~~Caught up into the geometry of the air~~
*   And*
~~But~~ *never had they stayed in their intent*

But for that woman's powerful character

Nor had the soul displayed its mastery in

All that is perplexed & withershin.

IV

Here student unknown traveller take your stand

When all the rooms & passages are gone

Withdraw your fancy from the foliage round

From that direct & easy moving sun

And dedicate—here amid fallen stone

That the briar & the nettle shade

A moment's memory to that sacred head.

Stanzas I, III, and IV are crossed out, and on page 34 there is
another draft of stanza III:

They came like swallows & like swallows went

Yet half a dozen in formation there
          That
Whirled and turned upon a compass point
               that
Because ~~a~~ woman's powerful character

~~*Had stayed a*~~

Could stay a swallow into first intent

Formed out of the charmed dreaming air

The intellectual sweetness of a line

The figure of a dance whirled withershin.

The poem's outline is now clear, although much polishing remains
to be done. In stanza II Yeats has withdrawn into modest anony-
mity, and altered 'We' to 'They' at the start of stanza III.

Stanzas I and IV advance a step nearer completion on page 35:

I

I meditate upon the swallow's flight,
          an aged
Upon ~~an ancient~~ woman & her house,

~~*Upon The the western sky luminous*~~

~~*The sycamore & lime tree*~~
                    lost
The sycamore & lime tree's ~~sunk~~ in night
          That   cloud is
~~*Although As*~~ *western ~~skies are~~ luminous;*

> Great work
> ~~On all~~ accomplished there in nature's spite
>
> For poets & for scholars after us,
>   *into*
> Thoughts long knitted to a single thought
>
> A dance like glory that those walls begot.

4.

> Here traveller, ~~po~~ scholar, poet take your stand
>
> When all those walls & passages are gone
>   While ~~nettles~~
> ~~And~~ nettles wave upon a shapeless mound
>   And   *broken*
> ~~Where the ash~~ sapling roots among the stone,
>   *bent*
> And dedicate—eyes ~~fixed~~ upon the ground
>   *Back turned*
> ~~Your back~~ upon the brightness of the sun
>   *the*
> And all the sensuality of shade—
>   *laurelled*
> A moment's memory to that ~~sacred~~ head.
>
>
> And dedicate upon this plot of ground
>
> Find though the walls & passages are gone
>
> The lime tree there will cast a pleasant shade
>
> A moment's memory &c.

The last four lines are no improvement, and wisely he crosses them out. On page 36 he works again at stanza III:

>   *They*
>   ~~Here all~~
> All came like swallows & like swallows went,
>
>
> Because that woman's powerful character
>
> Can make men execute what they intend

Crossing out the last two lines, he proceeds to a complete draft
of the stanza:

3.

> They came like swallows & like swallows went ;
>   And yet this
> ~~Because that~~ woman's powerful character
>
> Could keep a swallow to its first intent
>   ~~So~~ half a
> And   ~~Some~~ dozen in ~~com~~ formation here
>
> That seemed to whirl upon a compass point
>   those found imagined forms upon the
> ~~Formed out of the charmed dreaming air~~
>
> Found certainty upon the dreaming air
>
> The intellectual sweetness of those lines
>   Those   cut out
> ~~The~~ figures of a dance, ~~whirled~~ withershins

Below this he triumphantly seizes on the finished form of line 22:

> Found certainty upon the dreaming air

The swallows are now fully integrated into the poem. Their curious
flight is pin-pointed in the first line, and suggests the 'dance like
glory'. The walls of Coole may figuratively be said to have 'begotten' both the ordered dance of the birds and 'that famous
harmony' of men and one woman. Lady Gregory, whose epitaph
in fact this is, dominates the poem as she formerly dominated
Coole: she is the compass point at the centre of the circle. Only in
one stanza is she not mentioned, and it is a last-minute alteration,
which, in substituting 'laurelled' for 'sacred', deprives her of the
'odour of sanctity'.

So, after thirty-six pages of intensive working and correction,
Yeats comes at last to his manuscript fair copy:

Coole Park

I

I meditate upon a swallow's flight,

Upon an aged woman and her house,

A sycamore & lime tree lost in night

Although that western cloud is luminous,
        Great s constructed
~~*Great*~~ *work* ~~*accomplished*~~ *there in nature's spight*
        scholars
For ~~*scholars*~~ *& for poets after us,*

Thoughts long knitted into a single thought,

A dance like glory that those walls begot.

                        2

There Hyde before he had beaten into prose
                    Muses
That noble blade the ~~*muses*~~ *buckled on,*

There one that ruffled in a manly pose
                            slow
For all his timid heart, there that ~~*slow*~~ *man*

That meditative man John Synge & those

Impetuous men Shaw Taylor & Hugh Lane,

Found pride established in humility,

A scene well set, & excellent company.

                        3

They came like swallows & like swallows went,

And yet a woman's powerful character

Could keep a swallow to its first intent;

And half a dozen in formation there,

That seemed to whirl upon a compass point,

Found certainty upon the dreaming air,

The intellectual sweetness of those lines,

Those figures of a dance cut withershins.

4

> Page 38:   *Here*
> ~~*There poet*~~ *traveller, scholar poet take your stand*
>   *rooms*
> *When all those ~~walls~~ & passages are gone,*
>   *shapeless*
> *When nettles wave upon a ~~shapeless~~ mound*
>
> *And saplings root among the broken stone,*
>
> *And dedicate—eyes bent upon the ground,*
>
> *Back turned upon the brightness of the sun*
>
> *And all the sensuality of the shade—*
>
> *A moment's memory to that laurelled head.*

This is dated 'Dublin. Sept 7. 1929', as is also the one typescript of the poem in Mrs. Yeats's possession. Two changes of the definite to the indefinite article have softened the texture of the first stanza: 'the swallow' becomes 'a swallow', and 'the sycamore', 'a sycamore'. Still, however, the poem has one weak line, but the critical scalpel finds it before the first printing. The couplet ending stanza III:

> *The intellectual sweetness of those lines,*
>
> *Those figures of a dance cut withershins.*

was quoted in *Coole* (by Lady Gregory, Dublin, 1931) as:

> The intellectual sweetness of those lines,
> That can cross time and cut it withershins.

For *The Winding Stair and Other Poems* the improvement was carried still further, and the last line of the second stanza became finally: 'That cut through time or cross it withershins.' Few readers of this poem would guess that behind its comparatively simple structure and fluent rhythms lie thirty-eight pages of working—more than went to the making of any other poem that I know.

X

SEVEN SHORTER POEMS

• •

Memory

1. One had a lovely face,
2. And two or three had charm,
3. But charm and face were in vain
4. Because the mountain grass
5. Cannot but keep the form
6. Where the mountain hare has lain.

Consolation

1. O but there is wisdom
2. In what the sages said;
3. But stretch that body for a while
4. And lay down that head
5. Till I have told the sages
6. Where man is comforted.

7. How could passion run so deep
8. Had I never thought
9. That the crime of being born
10. Blackens all our lot?
11. But where the crime's committed
12. The crime can be forgot.

After Long Silence

1. Speech after long silence; it is right,
2. All other lovers being estranged or dead,
3. Unfriendly lamplight hid under its shade,
4. The curtains drawn upon unfriendly night,

5. That we descant and yet again descant
6. Upon the supreme theme of Art and Song:
7. Bodily decrepitude is wisdom; young
8. We loved each other and were ignorant.

The Nineteenth Century and After

1. Though the great song return no more
2. There's keen delight in what we have:
3. The rattle of pebbles on the shore
4. Under the receding wave.

The Results of Thought

1. Acquaintance; companion;
2. One dear brilliant woman;
3. The best-endowed, the elect,
4. All by their youth undone,
5. All, all, by that inhuman
6. Bitter glory wrecked.

7. But I have straightened out
8. Ruin, wreck and wrack;
9. I toiled long years and at length
10. Came to so deep a thought
11. I can summon back
12. All their wholesome strength.

13. What images are these,
14. That turn dull-eyed away,
15. Or shift time's filthy load,
16. Straighten aged knees,
17. Hesitate or stay?
18. What heads shake or nod?

An Acre of Grass

1. Picture and book remain,
2. An acre of green grass

3. For air and exercise,
4. Now strength of body goes;
5. Midnight, an old house
6. Where nothing stirs but a mouse.

7. My temptation is quiet.
8. Here at life's end
9. Neither loose imagination,
10. Nor the mill of the mind
11. Consuming its rag and bone,
12. Can make the truth known.

13. Grant me an old man's frenzy,
14. Myself must I remake
15. Till I am Timon and Lear
16. Or that William Blake
17. Who beat upon the wall
18. Till Truth obeyed his call;

19. A mind Michael Angelo knew
20. That can pierce the clouds,
21. Or inspired by frenzy
22. Shake the dead in their shrouds;
23. Forgotten else by mankind,
24. An old man's eagle mind.

A Bronze Head

1. Here at right of the entrance this bronze head,
2. Human, superhuman, a bird's round eye,
3. Everything else withered and mummy-dead.
4. What great tomb-haunter sweeps the distant sky
5. (Something may linger there though all else die;)
6. And finds there nothing to make its terror less
7. *Hysterica passio* of its own emptiness?

8. No dark tomb-haunter once; her form all full
9. As though with magnanimity of light,

10. Yet a most gentle woman; who can tell
11. Which of her forms has shown her substance right?
12. Or maybe substance can be composite,
13. Profound McTaggart thought so, and in a breath
14. A mouthful held the extreme of life and death.

15. But even at the starting-post, all sleek and new,
16. I saw the wildness in her and I thought
17. A vision of terror that it must live through
18. Had shattered her soul. Propinquity had brought
19. Imagination to that pitch where it casts out
20. All that is not itself: I had grown wild
21. And wandered murmuring everywhere, 'My child, my child!'

22. Or else I thought her supernatural;
23. As though a sterner eye looked through her eye
24. On this foul world in its decline and fall;
25. On gangling stocks grown great, great stocks run dry,
26. Ancestral pearls all pitched into a sty,
27. Heroic reverie mocked by clown and knave,
28. And wondered what was left for massacre to save.

YEATS'S mastery of poetic structure shows in his shorter poems no less than in those of four, five, or more stanzas. 'Memory', which was first published in February 1916, is a typical example. Delicate as a butterfly's wing, it must be handled lightly if its bloom is not to be rubbed away. It would seem also to have been captured like a butterfly, suddenly out of the air, and for once the lyrical spontaneity of Yeats's language appears to have been achieved without a struggle. At any rate there remains no trace of this on paper. The first draft has neither crossing-out nor correction, but it has one significant variation on the finished text. It reads:

> *One had a lovely face*
>
> *And two or three had charm*
>
> *But face & charm were in vain*
>
> *I could not change for the grass*
>
> *Cannot but keep the form*
>
> *Where the mountain hare has lain.*

Yeats, over fifty, is remembering some of the girls he had known as a young man. Hone says that the 'lovely face' was Olivia Shakespeare's:[1] he is probably right, but identities in this poem are less important than usual, because the poet's eyes look inward on himself, more than outward to *les dames du temps jadis*. 'Face & charm were in vain'. Why in vain? 'I could not change', he says; meaning, I think, that face and charm were not enough to sustain his permanent love, or make a more lasting mark upon his life and character than the hare makes upon the mountain.

The sheet of paper bearing this first draft has on its reverse a much-corrected version of 'The End of Day' (part IV of the sequence 'Upon a Dying Lady'). There is, however, a manuscript fair-copy of 'Memory' on a sheet of notepaper, headed:

[1] *W. B. Yeats, 1865–1939*, 1942, p. 113.

'18, Woburn Buildings, Upper Woburn Place, W.C.' Except for
minor changes of punctuation, it is the poem in its finished state:

> *One had a lovely face*
>
> *And two or three had charm*
>
> *But charm & face were in vain*
>
> *Because the mountain grass*
>
> *Cannot but keep the form*
>
> *Where the mountain hare has lain.*

'I could not change' has been cut out of line 4, and the meaning is
now implicit rather than explicit. We seem to have overheard
Yeats talking to himself, and although he is no longer directly mentioned, the apt and lovely metaphor of the last three lines perfectly
complements and illuminates the three that went before. Rhyme
and rhythm are muted to assist the meaning. Only in the last line
is this finally unfolded, and it is there clinched by the repetition
of 'mountain' and the one full rhyme (vain/lain). The metaphor
not only fits the theme as a glove fits a hand, but extends it by a
subtle innuendo. He says:

> *the mountain grass*
>
> *Cannot but keep the form*
>
> *Where the mountain hare has lain.*

But he knows, and his readers know, that the mountain grass cannot keep even the form indefinitely: in time face and charm will be
forgotten.

A second poem, which would seem to be associated with Mrs.
Shakespeare, since Yeats in a letter sent her an early draft of it, is
'Consolation'. There exists, however, an earlier and more revealing
manuscript than this: it is written in ink on a sheet of typing paper,
and reads:

> *~~I fathom~~ O but there is*
> *~~We fathomed all the~~ wisdom*
> *~~I know the wisdom that there is~~*
> *In what the sages said*
> *~~In all that you have~~ said*

But stretch ~~your~~ that body for a while

And lay down that head
                    to those
Till I have murmured ~~in your~~ ear
    ~~That~~
Where |~~How~~ life is comforted.

Never ~~had~~
~~How may~~ could
~~How could~~ passion run so deep
          it
Had ~~I~~ never thought

That the crime of being born
        Blackens
        ~~Blackened~~ all our lot

But where the crime's committed

The crime can be forgot.

When Yeats first put pen to paper he wrote:

I know the wisdom that there is

In all that you have said

This is a subtle opening, since it gives the reader the impression that he is overhearing a fragment of conversation between two lovers, and subsequently we are able to set the fragment into its context. The woman has said something to the effect that 'the crime of being born Blackens all our lot', and the poet is trying to comfort her. Correcting the first two lines, he makes them more objective:

We fathomed all the wisdom

In what the sages said

Finally he cuts out I/We/you altogether:

O but there is wisdom

In what the sages said

The sages are deliberately unspecified, but T. R. Henn detects in the last two lines of the poem an echo of Sophocles, and Yeats may here be thinking of those other Sophoclean lines, which he had himself translated (and incidentally sent to Mrs. Shakespeare four months previously).

Never to have lived is best, the ancient writers say;
Never to have drawn the breath of life, never to have looked into the
eye of day;

He admits that there is wisdom in such a view, but says that there is comfort to be had none the less:

How could passion run so deep

Had I never thought

That the crime of being born

Blackened all our lot

But where the crime's committed

The crime can be forgot.

In correcting this he again cuts out the subjective element, and in his letter to Mrs. Shakespeare on 23 June 1927 the second stanza reads:

How could passion run so deep

Had it never thought

That the crime of being born

Had blackened all our lot;

But where the crime's committed

The crime can be forgot.[1]

The passion is now Everyman's, but for the poem's first printing 'it' is changed back to 'I', in all probability because passion (by its nature) is incapable of thought. At the same time Yeats altered 'Had blackened' to the present tense 'Blackens', which better fits the other present-tense verbs, 'is committed' and 'can be forgot'.

[1] Wade, *Letters*, p. 726.

This last is a typical change, slight but perfectly correct. There are few other poems in which, having abandoned a subjective position for a more objective, he comes later to reverse his decision.

Another poem originating, it would seem, from Yeats's memories of Olivia Shakespeare, makes its first, prose, appearance on page 69 of Manuscript Book B. This is headed simply 'Subject', and reads:

> *Your hair is white*
>
> *My hair is white*
>
> *Come let us talk of love*
>
> *What other theme do we know*
>
> *When we were young*
>
> *We were in love with one another*
>
> *And therefore ignorant*

The intimate, conversational tone of the prose draft is continued when the poem is cast, after a few preliminary jottings, in a verse mould on page 73:

> ~~*I k*~~
>
> *Once more I have kissed your hair & it is right—*
>
> *All other lovers being estranged or dead*
>
> ~~*The heavy curtains drawn   the candle light*~~
>
> ~~*Bringing a doubtful (   ) with the shade*~~
>
>   *discant*
> ~~*We call our wisdom up upon our wisdom & descant*~~
>
> ~~*Upon the supreme theme of art & song*~~
>
> *Decrepitude increases wisdom—young*
>
> *We loved each other & were ignorant*

A general reflection on ignorance and wisdom is here introduced to a highly personal and subjective setting. On the facing page 72

Yeats works over the unsatisfactory lines 3–6, and rejects two new versions of line 3:

> *And shutters clapped upon the deepening night*

and

> *Those curtains drawn upon the deepening night.*

The final version of 'After Long Silence', dated 'Nov 1929' on page 75, begins on a more dignified and objective note. The poet no longer speaks in the first person singular, and all reference to hair has vanished:

> *Speech after long silence; it is right—*
>
> *All other lovers being estranged or dead,*
>   *hid*
> *Unfriendly lamp-light ~~hid~~ under its shade,*
>   *upon*
> *The curtains drawn ~~upon~~ unfriendly night—*
>
> *That we descant & yet again descant*
>
> *Upon the supreme theme of art and song:*
>
> *Bodily decrepitude is wisdom; young*
>
> *We loved each other & were ignorant*

The private voice has changed to a public voice. The first quatrain, with its suspension strikingly emphasized by the repetition of 'unfriendly', is now almost as objective as the statement of the last two lines. This has been at once expanded and compressed by the insertion of 'Bodily' before 'decrepitude', and by the alteration of 'increases' to the more paradoxical 'is'. The poem is now a more compact artistic whole, but the personal element is so reduced that without knowledge of the early drafts one could not even say whether a man or a woman were speaking.

Ellmann tells us that the quatrain named after *The Nineteenth Century and After* review was written between January and 2 March 1929.[1] At first, apparently Yeats intended it to come third in a lyrical sequence to 'At Algeciras—A Meditation upon Death', and 'Mohini Chatterjee'. His intention, however, was not to be fulfilled.

---

[1] *The Identity of Yeats*, 1954, p. 266.

> Between the conception
> And the creation
> Between the emotion
> And the response
> Falls the shadow.

Whereas the first two poems in the sequence investigate the possibility of a future life after the death of the body, 'The Nineteenth
Century and After' is concerned with the present in relation to the
past. It is true that 'the pebbles on the shore' may be drawn from
the same level of memory as the 'actual shells of Rosses' level
shore', but there the resemblance ends.

Ellmann quotes the first draft as follows:

> *Though the great men return no more*
>
> *I take delight in what I have:*
>
> *The rattle of pebbles on the shore*
>
> *Under the outgoing wave.*

He deduces from the vague phrase, 'great men', that Yeats did not
at first limit the quatrain's applicability to 'poets dead and gone'.
If he did not; and if 'great men' included also statesmen, generals,
lawgivers, &c.,

> *The rattle of pebbles on the shore*
>
> *Under the outgoing wave.*

had only the barest metaphorical meaning. That from the start
he had only poets in mind, is, I think, proved by his letter to Olivia
Shakespeare, dated 'March 2' (1929). The relevant passage reads:

I have turned from Browning—to me a dangerous influence—to
Morris and read through his *Defence of Guenevere* and some unfinished
prose fragments with great wonder. I have come to fear the world's
last great poetic period is over.

> Though the great song return no more
> There's keen delight in what we have—
> A rattle of pebbles on the shore
> Under the receding wave.

The young do not feel like that—George does not, nor Ezra—but men
far off feel it—in Japan for instance.[1]

---

[1] Wade, *Letters*, p. 759.

Browning and Morris would seem to have prompted the poem. Beside them, I suggest, Yeats found the voice of contemporary poetry no more significant than 'The rattle of pebbles on the shore'. This he makes much more explicit in the second version, where 'the great song' (instead of 'men') provides a contrast to the lesser noise of the pebbles. His original, wholly subjective statement: 'I take delight in what I have' which might have been regarded as no more than a freakish opinion, becomes, when presented objectively, seemingly authoritative: 'There's keen delight in what we have—'. Temporarily he alters 'The rattle' to 'A rattle', and in the last line changes the epithet, 'outgoing', to the much smoother 'receding'.

Wave and tide metaphors are common in Yeats's later poetry: for example, 'The blood-dimmed tide' ('The Second Coming'), and 'this filthy modern tide' ('The Statues'). They are generally related to his theories of the interlocking gyres, which have a similar fluctuating movement. So in 'The Nineteenth Century and After', the 'receding wave' refers both to the diminished sound of modern poetry, and to the objective era which must ebb before the new subjective 'wave' can roll in again. Small though the poem is, Yeats has 'loaded every rift with ore'.

Manuscript Book C contains an interesting example of his restless manner of composition. What appears to be the beginning of the poem later entitled 'The Results of Thought' is to be found on page 170:

> *I have unravelled all*
>
> *The fullness & the lack*
>
> *That set our minds astray*
>
> *That woman there I call*
> *those*
> *Call ~~old~~ companies back*
> *~~or to~~*
> *To peace & sanity.*

The emphasis at first is on himself, who has 'unravelled all', and 'That woman' (presumably Maud Gonne) is of only secondary importance. By the time he reached the first complete draft, on

page 235, however, their relative positions had been reversed, and
it is the poet's friends who are at the centre of the poem. First to be
written were the stanzas at the left-hand side of the page, all of
which he later crossed out with vertical lines.

At last

Friends ignorant & blind	*Acquaintance or companion;*
Wrecked lives, a woman there	*One dear, brilliant woman;*
Of all wrecks there the worst	*The best endowed; the elect,*
A dear beloved mind	*All by their youth undone*
Thinks of its despair	*All, all by that inhuman*
There by its youth acurst	*Bitter glory wrecked.*

I have unravelled all	*But I have unravelled all*
Uncovered all the	
The ~~fulness~~ & the lack	*Discovered all the lack*
That set our wits astray	
That woman there I call	
Call those companies back	
To peace & ~~sanity~~ sanity	

Discoloured images,	
~~Carry on~~ Pass on	
~~Driven on~~ their separate ways	
Under	
~~Turn~~ discoloured loads	*~~Shift their filthy loads~~*
~~Straighten the aged knees~~	
~~Pass, or st~~	
Or straighten aged knees	
Hesitate & gaze	
A head shakes or nods.	

What images are these?   ~~Whi~~ That
   ~~Go~~
~~That pass on separate ways~~   ~~That~~ turn dull eyed away

   ~~Under time's filthy load~~   Or shift time's filthy load
Some   And
   ~~Or~~ straighten aged knees,   Hesitate or stay

~~Hesitate & gaze~~

~~What head shake or nods~~   What heads shake or nod

Still dissatisfied with the second stanza, Yeats returns to it on the left-hand page (234):

      straightened
But I have ~~ravelled~~ out
  the
All ~~the~~ wreck & rack

Of that gay company.

After long years my ~~thought,~~ thought
   Call & calls it
~~Can summon~~ it back

~~To For~~ From insanity.

~~Found words to call it summon it back~~
  ~~From insanity~~
      years
I toiled long ~~years~~ & at length

~~Found such deep thought~~   Have found such a deep thought
  That I call this back
~~I can call it back~~

From ~~its~~ insanity

Into their wholesome strength

The workings on this page have again been crossed out with a vertical line, but they have brought the stanza one stage nearer its final shape, and almost every correction is an improvement.

Yeats is never afraid to make a radical alteration when the situation demands it. Of the first draft of stanza I, on page 235, he

salvages not a rhyme, but completely recasts his material and re-
places six flat, undistinguished lines with six that are taut and
vibrant. The striking repetition of 'all' drives the verse forward
to a climactic oxymoron, 'bitter glory'. The opening of stanza II
picks up the word 'wreck': this, says the poet, he can at last
straighten out, and the stanza ends on a rising note of hope and
expectation—deliberate, but false. Stanza III, cast, as in its first
draft on page 235, as a statement, is a considerable anticlimax; but
as a question (or, more correctly, two questions) it manages to
convey all of the poet's surprise and horror at his ugly revelation.
The 'gay company' have obeyed his summons, but are—like himself—gay and beautiful no longer.

A first fair copy appears on page 237, and is dated 'August 18'
(1931): it is untitled:

> *Acquaintance ; companion ;*
>
> *One dear brilliant woman ;*
>
> *The best endowed ; the elect ;*
>
> *All by their youth undone,*
>
> *All all by that inhuman*
>
> *Bitter glory wrecked.*

> *Have I not*
> *~~But I have~~ straightened out*
> *That great*
> *~~All this~~ wreck and wrack?*

> *I toiled long years & at length*
> *   came to so deep a*
> *~~Found such a deep~~ thought*
> *   That   summon*
> *I can ~~call them~~ back*
> *   All*
> *~~Into~~ their wholesome strength*

> *What images are these*
>
> *That turn dull-eyed away*

> *Or shift Time's filthy load,*
>
> *Straighten aged knees,*
>
> *Hesitate & stay?*
>
> *What heads shake or nod?*

Also on 18 August Yeats turned back to page 155, and there made another fair copy (at first entitled 'After long years') incorporating the corrections to stanza II. Even then he had not finished, for when the poem first appeared in print, that stanza began:

> But I have straightened out
> All the wreck and wrack;

The rhetorical interrogative is now reserved for stanza III. At the second printing line 8 was altered to: 'Ruin, wreck and wrack;' and line 11, 'I could summon back', became—more effectively—'I can summon back'. Finally, what I take to be a misprint was emended in line 3, 'The endowed, the elect;' became—as it had been in every manuscript draft—'The best-endowed, the elect,'.

An unusual aspect of Yeats's character is revealed in the development of 'An Acre of Grass'. The one manuscript, on a loose-leaf sheet of paper, is untitled; and the many corrections and small, neat writing of the first two stanzas suggest that the poem began slowly:

> *I*
>
> ~~*My*~~ *picture & ~~books~~ remain*
>   *An*   *green*
> ~~*For*~~ *acre of ~~hills &~~ grass,*
>
> ~~*Good for sufficient exercise*~~ *For air & exercise*
>
> ~~*Now that health goes*~~ *Now strength of body goes*
>
> *Midnight, an old house*
>
> *Where nothing stirs but a mouse*

Here the most significant alteration is the dropping of 'My' in the first line, which instantly converts a subjective stanza into an objective one, or at any rate into one in which the poet is not directly mentioned. Though clearly his voice is speaking, the man —as distinct from Everyman grown old—appears first in stanza II:

II

~~All tem~~
~~Meditation is my temptation~~   *My temptation is quiet*
            life's end
Now ~~the last chill~~ draws near
    ~~No~~ neither loose
~~Yet by loose~~ reverie
            those
Nor by ~~those~~ thoughts that hear

Dry bone grind dry bone
    Make
Can truth ~~be~~ known

The original version of line 7, 'Meditation is my temptation', an unpleasant jingle, yet suggests that in his revision Yeats intended 'quiet' as a noun, and not an adjective, as it is sometimes interpreted.

With stanza III the tempo of composition would seem to have quickened: there is only one correction and the writing runs more boldly:

II

Grant me an old man's frenzy
        That
~~Till~~ I myself re-make;

Till I am Timon & Lear

And that William Blake

Who beat upon the wall

Till Truth obeyed his call;

The 'Till' of line 14, of course, is removed because of the two later lines, which begin in the same fashion. Stanza IV was written at even higher pressure than stanza III, and so fast did the pen pass over the paper that several words are linked together.

IV

A mind Michael Angelo knew

That can pierce the clouds

Or inspired by frenzy

Shake the dead in their shrouds

Forgotten else by mankind

An old man's eagle mind

Fs. 2 and 3 are identical carbon typescripts, copied with only slight variation from the manuscript and with corrections in pencil. Stanza II on F. *2r* reads:

My temptation is quiet

Now life's end draws near;
Neither loose reverie
Nor those thoughts that ~~hear~~ *grind*
                              upon
Dry bone ~~grind~~ dry bone

Can make the truth known.

At the foot of this page he wrote a bold 'P.T.O.', which was followed on F. *2v* by the following manuscript stanzas:

At first we seemed a ~~(——)~~
~~*We seemed like any*~~ *married pair*

That on the feathers lay

But twas no matter what we were

I am true to Billy Boy

He lay upon me head to tail
~~*He*~~
~~*And*~~ *wriggled in his joy*

But it was all of no avail

I am true to Billy Boy

> *When he stood me*
> *He ~~put me~~ in ~~standing~~ on my head*
> *I did him sore annoy*
> *~~And thought I must be shy~~*
>
> *Because I cared not what he did*
>
> *Being true to Billy Boy*

This descent from the sublime to the ridiculous needs no critical
comment. It is perhaps over-pompous even to mention the popular
ballad 'Billy Boy', which may have been at the back of his mind,
and its relevance to his own Christian name. There have been
composed many impromptu ballads bawdier and funnier than this,
but it is amusing to see how quickly Yeats switches back from the
ridiculous to the sublime.

Stanza II on (typescript) F. 3*r* shows a most brilliant correction:

My temptation is quiet

~~Now life's end draws near~~	*Here at life's end*
~~Neither loose reverie~~	*Neither loose imagination*
~~Nor those thoughts that hear~~	*Nor the mill of the mind*
~~Dry bone grind dry bone~~	*Consuming its rag & bone*

Can make the truth known.

The splendid image of 'The mill of the mind' was no doubt
prompted by his thinking of 'that William Blake' to whose influence
in earlier years he owed so much.

In a later typescript (F. 4) line 14, 'That I myself remake' is
changed to 'Myself must I remake', which was to be the final
reading, although for the first two printings the line was, 'Myself I
must remake'. This had been foreshadowed by the terse stanza
published in the *Collected Works* (1908):

> The friends that have it I do wrong
> Whenever I remake a song,
> Should know what issue is at stake:
> It is myself that I remake.

Similarly, the vivid 'rag and bone' phrase in 'An Acre of Grass'
would seem to foreshadow 'the rag-and-bone shop of the heart.'
in 'The Circus Animals' Desertion'.

The last poem that I mean to consider in this section is 'A Bronze Head', occasioned by Laurence Campbell's bronze-painted plaster bust of Maud Gonne, in the Dublin Municipal Gallery.

Yeats's first, unrhymed draft addresses the head as if it were Maud Gonne herself:

> ~~I come upon you~~
>
> I ~~pass~~ the
>   on the right of the entrance (   )
> ~~I found the bronze on the right of the great door~~
>
> ~~In human superhuman terrible~~
>
> ~~That bronze inhuman super, human~~
>
> I found that human super human head

This he crossed out, and began again, on a less personal note:

> I found on right of the entrance the bronze head
>   A bird's great eyes
> Human superhuman. ~~Great round~~ eyes
>
> ~~Like a bird's eye all else withered & mummified~~
>
> ~~All else everything else withered & mummy dead~~
>
> All else there withered & mummy dead
>
> A gaze that has swept the dark skies

Having reached the bottom of the page, he squeezes in at the top, and on the slant, a draft of the stanza's last four lines:

> What bird of prey has swept the west skies
>   darkening
> What great tomb haunter has swept the ~~west~~ skies
>
> And there it remains while all else dies
>
> And finds there nothing to make its terror less
>
> Histerica Passio of its own emptiness

It would seem from the surviving manuscripts as if there was almost no intermediate stage between this and a full draft of the poem sufficiently close to the final text as to make transcription unnecessary. Professor Jeffares, however, has been guilty of a most uncharacteristic mis-transcription,[1] which must be corrected. The stanza which he says Yeats dropped from the manuscript of 'A Bronze Head', was never a part of that poem at all, but rather the fifth and last stanza of 'The Circus Animals' Desertion' (originally entitled 'Despair On the Lack of a Theme'). It persisted even into the typescript stage, and read:

> O hour of triumph come and make me gay!
>
> If burnished chariots are put to flight
>
> Why brood upon old triumph, prepare to die;
>
> Even at the approach of the un-imaged night
>
> Man has the refuge of his gaity;
>
> A dab of black enhances every white,
>
> Tension is but the vigour of the mind,
>
> Cannon the god and father of mankind.

Even discounting the conclusive manuscript proof, this is clearly more in tune with 'The Circus Animals' Desertion' than with 'A Bronze Head'. In this Yeats removes all mention of himself from stanza I, lest his shadow, as it were, should interfere with the poem's dominant image. Only in stanzas III and IV does the commentator appear, and never could he have so lost his sense of structure as to introduce a wholly subjective stanza. This is a poem about Maud Gonne alive and dead, and alive-in-death, and its unity is its strength.

[1] *W. B. Yeats/Man and Poet*, 1949, p. 294.

XI

THE BLACK TOWER

1. Say that the men of the old black tower,
2. Though they but feed as the goatherd feeds,
3. Their money spent, their wine gone sour,
4. Lack nothing that a soldier needs,
5. That all are oath-bound men:
6. Those banners come not in.

7. *There in the tomb stand the dead upright,*
8. *But winds come up from the shore:*
9. *They shake when the winds roar,*
10. *Old bones upon the mountain shake.*

11. Those banners come to bribe or threaten,
12. Or whisper that a man's a fool
13. Who, when his own right king's forgotten,
14. Cares what king sets up his rule.
15. If he died long ago
16. Why do you dread us so?

17. *There in the tomb drops the faint moonlight,*
18. *But wind comes up from the shore:*
19. *They shake when the winds roar,*
20. *Old bones upon the mountain shake.*

21. The tower's old cook that must climb and clamber
22. Catching small birds in the dew of the morn
23. When we hale men lie stretched in slumber
24. Swears that he hears the king's great horn.
25. But he's a lying hound:
26. Stand we on guard oath-bound!

27. *There in the tomb the dark grows blacker,*
28. *But wind comes up from the shore:*
29. *They shake when the winds roar,*
30. *Old bones upon the mountain shake.*

•••

IN January 1939 Yeats lay on his death-bed in the south of France. From the sick-room window at Cap Martin he looked out towards Roquebrune with its graveyard-covered slopes rising to the church of Saint Pancras at its summit. He must have been reminded of that other Saint Pancras in London, in whose shadow he had lived at Woburn Buildings. Now dying on the Riviera he found, I suspect, in this view the stimulus for his last poem. 'The Black Tower' is dated 21 January, and on the 28th the poet died.

There are in Mrs. Yeats's possession eleven loose-leaf sheets of manuscript and a single corrected typescript. There is in the National Library, Dublin, one further page of manuscript among the drafts of *The Death of Cuchulain*, a play on which Yeats was also working at the time of his death. The handwriting throughout is that of an old, myopic, and dying man.

F. 1r is a prose draft:

I

of the black tower
I speak for the ~~gyres~~ gyres

~~Of the black tower (━━━━━━) go~~

~~We form no alliance~~

You are not of our kin ~~so begone~~

~~We form no alliance we need no help~~

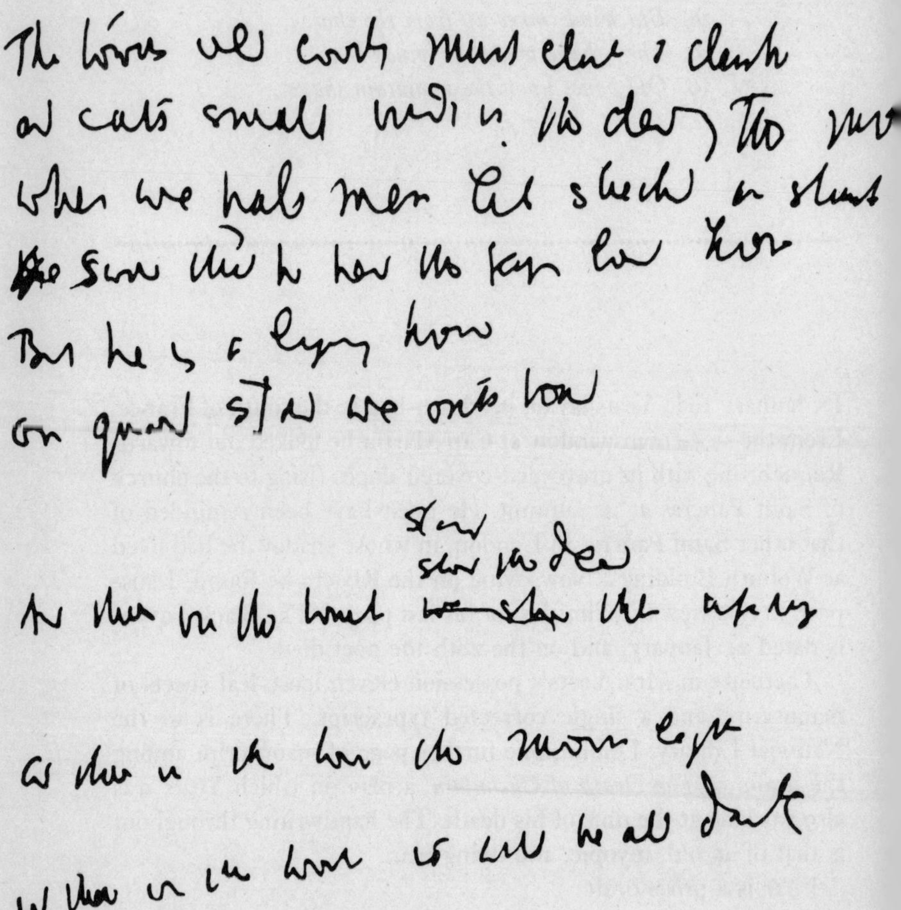

F. 5*v* of 'The Black Tower': see page 240 for transcription.

F. 6r of 'The Black Tower': see page 233 for transcription.

The Gods have brought us milk & flesh

Nothing remains to us but this

But this high lonely place

Begone you are not oath bound

The old tower

2

He we that we await will come

You say that he died long ago

Say what you will

~~sworn~~ *sworn*

We have ~~sworn~~ & we wait.

We need no help, we seek no allies

We love this barren spot

Old tower

3

The poem's basic situation begins to emerge. The inmates of a black tower prefer their present independence to a proffered, and it may be profitable, alliance to another power not of their kin. They await the return of someone who died long ago. The figure 3 at the foot of this page shows that Yeats had a further stanza in his head at this stage, but there is no prose draft of it that I have seen. On F. 1r he makes no attempt to disguise his voice. 'I speak for the gyres of the black tower'. By 'gyres' he means primarily, I think, the 'winding, gyring, spiring treadmill of a stair'. On behalf of the inmates of the tower—'we'—he addresses the alien forces: 'You are not of our kin'. This is expanded on F. 1v:

We thank your king in the name of the tower

~~We men that would have all that we need~~
it has
~~But we have all that soldiers need~~

~~We make no hard bargain~~

~~But make no~~

But it has all that we soldiers need

It makes no bargain—great its power

Although we feed as the goatherds feed

⟨————————————————⟩

~~And this a~~

| | ~~and the oath b~~ | And we outlaws are few |
| And seems (|) a desolate home, | We laugh because we knew |

~~Though we that secret know~~

(   )

~~Our fathers stand among the rocks~~

~~Winds make an old bone shake~~

~~It blow from the black pigs~~

~~Our fathers stand among the rocks~~

~~But winds can the old bones shake~~

~~When it old blows from the black pig's dike~~

Mrs. Yeats's statement that this is a poem 'on the subject of political propaganda'[1] already begins to make sense. The tower symbol has gathered associations like a snowball, until it is here only Thoor Ballylee in so far as Thoor Ballylee is a microcosm of Ireland. 'In the name of the tower' the poet thanks a second king for his offer of assistance, and declines it. On the political plane this can only be the king of England. The Irish are soldiers: Yeats could never forget the heroic ideal. They are outlaws that 'feed as the goatherd feeds', but they have a secret that enables them to reject the overtures of England. This, I take it, is the knowledge that their king

[1] G. B. Saul, *Prolegomena to the Study of Yeats's Poems*, 1957, p. 176.

will return. On a literal plane this could mean one of the high
kings of Cashel, ancient rulers of Ireland, who might come back
like Arthur from Avalon to release his people from bondage. On a
more simple and figurative plane it could mean that the dormant
spirit of Ireland will awake and inspire the people to attain their
former dignity and power.

This is made clearer by the reference to 'the black pig's dike'.
On this allusion to folk-lore, Yeats himself supplies us with the
relevant gloss in connexion with a poem written before the turn of
the century, and entitled 'The Valley of the Black Pig'. His note I
quote in full:

The Irish peasantry have for generations comforted themselves, in
their misfortunes, with visions of a great battle, to be fought in a
mysterious valley called, 'The Valley of the Black Pig', and to break
at last the power of their enemies. A few years ago, in the barony of
Lisadell, in county Sligo, an old man would fall entranced upon the
ground from time to time, and rave out a description of the battle;
and I have myself heard said that the girths shall rot from the bellies of
the horses, because of the few men that shall come alive out of the
valley.[1]

Again, he writes in one of the tales in *The Celtic Twilight*:

Presently our talk of war shifted, as it had a way of doing, to the
battle of the Black Pig, which seems to her a battle between Ireland and
England, but to me an Armageddon which shall quench all things in
the Ancestral Darkness again.[2]

What were at first 'old bones . . . among the rocks' are now more
specifically 'Our fathers': these are the ancient heroic dead. They
do not lie in their graves, but stand. It has been suggested that
Yeats was thinking of the old Irish warrior, Eoghan Bel, who after
the battle of Sligo in 537 was buried in an upright position, with
his red javelin in hand and pointing out to sea. This is, I think, too
specific. He had in mind a common Irish practice, that he may have
heard of for the first time in *Ancient Cures, Charms & Usages of
Ireland*[3] by Lady Wilde. I have seen the poet's own marked and

---

[1] *Variorum*, p. 161.   [2] *Collected Works*, 1908, vol. v, p. 154.   [3] 1890 edition.

annotated copy of this book. There are pencil marks on the last page (p. 256), which make it certain that he read the last paragraph. This I give in full:

There was also another mode of burial for warriors. The dead were placed in a standing position, their arms and shield beside them, and a great circular cairn of earth and stones was raised over them. Thus the heroic king of Munster slain in battle, was placed in his grave. 'Mogha-Neid lies in his sepulchre, with his javelin by his shoulder, with his club which was strong in battle, with his helmet, with his sword; long shall he be lamented with deep love, and his absence be the cause of darkest sorrow.'

A reader new to Yeats and new to Irish folk-lore might be forgiven for wondering how the wind can make bones shake, which are presumably underground. Yeats again supplies the answer in his note to an earlier poem, this time 'The Hosting of the Sidhe':

The powerful and wealthy called the gods of ancient Ireland the Tuatha De Danaan, or the tribes of the goddess Danu, but the poor called them, and still sometimes call them, the Sidhe, from Aes Sidhe or Sluagh Sidhe, the people of the Faery Hills, as these words are usually explained. Sidhe is also Gaelic for wind, and certainly the Sidhe have much to do with the wind. They journey in whirling winds, the winds that were called the dance of the daughters of Herodias in the Middle Ages, Herodias doubtless taking the place of some old goddess. When the country people see the leaves whirling on the road they bless themselves, because they believe the Sidhe to be passing by.[1]

The Gods of ancient Ireland then inspire the bones of the heroic dead, reminding them of the valley or dyke of the black pig, where their ultimate victorious battle is to be fought.

The manuscript leaves being now detached from the original notebook, it is impossible to order them with any certainty; to say whether stanza I was written before stanza II, or the refrain before either. Mrs. Yeats says that he worked to no definite pattern, but passed haphazardly from stanza to stanza and back again, as the spirit moved him. The best I can do is to assume that he wrote the stanzas in their final order. There are in all four drafts of the first stanza. One I have given already. F. 2r is still very rough:

[1] *Variorum*, p. 800.

Say that the men in this old

~~goat~~   Lack nothing that a soldier

~~Say that the men that keep this~~

~~Go Towns men & say that the~~ men of the tower
    have got all that
~~Have Lack that~~ a soldier needs

~~That they lack (   ), & their wine gone sour~~

That their (   ) is gone & their wine gone sour

And they but feed as the goat herd feed s

~~(   ) This desolate spot their home~~

~~Here on this spot we stay~~ Oath bound men & we stay

Not of our kin are they ~~Go for your work is~~
              ~~Go for your~~ task is done   our
~~Go You are not our kin Was~~ & They say they are not ~~your~~ kin

*   You are not of our kin

*   That banner comes not in

            stand
Our fathers ~~are buried~~ upright in ~~the tomb~~ their tomb
    But
~~Wind~~ Wind comes from the shore

And they shake when the winds roar

~~Among the mountain rocks they shake~~

Old bones upon the mountain shake

Old bones shake upon the mountain

            ~~or among~~ the

F. 3r is as follows:

We thank the towns men in the name of the Tower
    it has
Say ~~we have~~ all that soldiers need

Why should it bargain great its power

Although we feed as the goatherds feed

* Denotes a line inserted from the foot of the page.

~~Say to~~

Say

Go to the men of the black pig's banner
     That
~~Say~~ we have all that a soldier needs
          Though is spent & the wine is bitter
~~Though the wine is sour bitter & the bran spent~~

And we but feed as the goat herds feed

This desolate shore is our home

No talk can make us come

          The   ⟨——————⟩ our fathers stand upright in the
~~Old bones upon the mountain~~
          Which   ~~the~~ wind comes from the shore
But ~~shake when the wind roars~~

~~Up from the sea shore~~

They shake with the winds' roar
                                        mountain
~~The old bones shake upon the mountain among the rocks~~
The old bones upon the mountain shake

On F. 5r the 'towns men' have disappeared, but there is still reference to 'the black pig's dyke':

~~Who stands~~

~~Begone from this by the old black tower~~
                    this ancient ⟨——⟩ ~~this dark~~ wall
I thank you in name of ~~the black tower~~
                    the ancient tower
          is not a thing
But there is ~~nothing~~ that we need

~~You that you whe~~ We know that your king (   ) & proud

And we but feed as the goat herds feed

Our fathers stand in the tomb upright

But wind makes an old bone shake

> *When it blows from the black pig's dyke*
>
> *Our fathers stand in the tomb up right*

The next time that this stanza appears is in the first composite draft: but before advancing to stanza II, two fragments must be considered since they are on the reverse of early drafts of this poem. I quote them in the order arranged by Mrs. Yeats. F. 3*v*:

> *Think all a vision of the air*
>
> *But they will soon be merely this*
>
> *Not yet my son not yet*
>
> *For this is no regret*
>
> *When ghosts & dreams walk by*

F. 4*v* is only a little less chaotic, and its final words are written in the wildest scrawl:

> *What is out there,* (――――) *those*
>
> ~~*What men are these that pass in the skies*~~
>
> *A dream* ~~*by God*~~ *of the day to go*
>
> *That work all done & well*
>
> *Do I dream this sound in the sky*
>
> *Do you hear* (   ) *father*
>   *no no*
> ~~*no no*~~   *not yet   not yet*
>
> *But* (   )
>
>   *soon soon   my son*

'He knew he was dying', said Mrs. Yeats; and though we shall probably never know the exact thought that caused this most moving digression, it would seem that the dead 'fathers' among the rocks may have prompted one who was himself a father, and dying, to address his own son in words as old as David's lament for Absalom.

There appear to be two drafts of the second stanza before the poem is put together as a whole. F. 6r shows the poet thinking on paper:

> ~~You~~ say that
>
> ~~You We & this no master~~
>
> ~~Who say that our king is dead~~
>   ~~that~~
> ~~They say our destruction is when~~ (   )
>
> ~~You say that we're~~
>
> ~~You say that the tower's master be forgotten~~
>
> ~~& we but left master less we~~
>
> ~~They lie that say our king has forgot~~
>
> ~~They lie that say we are forgotten~~
>
> You call us crazed men & forgotten
>
> ⟨————————————————⟩
>
> That is some law that no one knows
>
> He has long laid dead & (   )
>
> Then why do you dread us so

On F. 2v the stanza begins to take shape, and the alien power is no longer addressed as 'you' but 'they':

> They think that they can buy us
>   And
> ~~Yet~~ say that our dead

Then after five lines of chaotic scribbling Yeats continues:

> They sent a messenger to buy us
>   They (   )
> ~~Say we were lost & our king dead~~
>
> That all we need is an alliance
>   ~~That~~
> Offer us those great affairs

Should we accept that law instead

If he died long ago

Why do they hate us so

At this point we are forced to ask ourselves who is the messenger. Subjectively, he might represent the temptation of atheistic rationalism that denies the God in which Old Tom (see stanza III below) believes. On the England–Ireland level the messenger may simply represent the British Government. There is a further area of interpretation which must have been in Yeats's mind in 1939: the wider international one. The shadows of the Nazi banners were extending over Europe, and on this plane the messenger comes from Hitler.

Prior to the first full draft there are three sheets of working on stanza III whose precise order of composition is difficult to fix, but it is not important. F. 6*v* is brief:

There is an old man that goes out clambering
   ⟨————⟩ *snaring small birds for his cooking pot*
While ~~all~~ ⟨————⟩ *all sound men lie slumbering*

That say he's a lying hound

~~Who stand here the oath bound~~

He stand the oath bound

Fs. 7*r* and 8*r* are more revealing. F. 7*r*, which has workings from *The Death of Cuchulain* on its verso, reads:

The old bones shake among the rocks

They stand upright there

And the wind roars up from the shore

The old bones shake among the rocks

———————

3.

Old Tom said he has
      he has heard upon the hill
He has heard it before dawn

But is crazy because of his age

And (   ) with nothing

But we are oath-bound & we (   )

                    that
Our cook goes for to climb & clamber

And catch small birds in the dew of the morn

~~*When decent men prefer their slumber*~~/*better men lie stretched in*

Says that he heard the king's low horn

But he is a lying hound

F. 8*r* is similar:

Old Tom ~~*our cook*~~ *upon the rock must clamber*

~~*To snare small birds for our cooking pot*~~

~~*When young men when we hale men are stretched in slumber*~~

~~*And sets his snare & catches a bird*~~

                    the rough rock
Old Tom that over ~~*rocks*~~ *must clamber s*

~~*To snare his birds between night & morn*~~

~~*Snare small birds between night & morn*~~

~~*From For*~~ *For birds & eggs before night & morn*

When all hale men prefer their slumber
                    king's great horn
Swears he ~~*has heard our master's*~~ *horn*
        I think he's
But ~~*he is*~~ *a lying hound*
        But
~~*He stands*~~ *Here stand we the oath bound*

But here

These drafts show the inmates of the tower to be waiting for a king whose horn the cook claims to have heard. The poet's counter-assertion 'But he is a lying hound' is for some reason not wholly convincing: we are secretly inclined to believe the cook, and, I submit, it is intended that we should. Another character, who eventually merges with the cook, is Old Tom who has heard something upon the hill, and before dawn. That something is clearly the horn; yet again we hear the sceptical voice of the poet: 'But [he] is crazy because of his age'.

Who is Old Tom? I think it not improbable that Yeats had been impressed by the dramatic possibilities in Shakespeare's Poor Tom, the sane man aping the fool upon the heath. The mask of Old Tom is one of the many through which the poet speaks. Tom the Lunatic had said in an earlier poem:

> Whatever stands in field or flood,
> Bird, beast, fish or man,
> Mare or stallion, cock or hen,
> Stands in God's unchanging eye
> In all the vigour of its blood;
> In that faith I live or die.

Number XXIII of the 'Words for Music Perhaps' is entitled 'Tom at Cruachan', and number XXI, 'The Dancer at Cruachan and Cro-Patrick'. Although Tom is not mentioned in the latter, clearly he it is who says:

> I, proclaiming that there is
> Among birds or beasts or men
> One that is perfect or at peace,
> Danced on Cruachan's windy plain,
> Upon Cro-Patrick sang aloud;
> All that could run or leap or swim
> Whether in wood, water or cloud,
> Acclaiming, proclaiming, declaiming Him.

This Tom is the wise fool, and more Christian than lunatic, or it may be that Yeats is deliberately equating the two. I believe myself that Tom represents the Christian in Yeats, whom he could never entirely suppress, and struggled with particularly, Mrs. Yeats told me, when he was ill. If Tom is waiting for the horn of somebody, a king, who died long ago, the king may be Christ and the horn related to the trumpets that sound on the other side. A symbolic

poem such as 'The Black Tower' does not have one meaning but
several. I would not press this subjective interpretation too strongly,
since a more objective meaning is quite clearly the dominant one;
but their co-existence is not only possible but desirable if the poem
is to make its 'full, perfect and sufficient' impact on the reader.

I come now to the first composite draft of the poem on Fs. 8v,
9r, and 10r. Arrows show quite clearly that in the original notebook 8v and 9r faced each other; 9r being on the right. It reads as
follows:

The watch men

Say that the men in the old Tower
           the
Lack nothing that ~~a~~ soldier needs
    Their
~~Though~~ money is spent & ~~the bread~~ their wine gone sour

~~That~~ And they but feed as the goat herd feeds

But this banner comes not in

Because not of our kin

Our fathers stand upright in the tomb

But wind comes up from the shore

They shake when the winds roar
      upon
Old bones ~~on~~ the mountain shake

They have sent their messenger to buy us
   ~~And leave~~   ~~men swear that~~
And ~~some that have sworn that~~ our king is dead

Their leave proof that our king is dead

What we lack is their alliance

Their messenger has come to buy us

~~To proof that our king is dead~~

To bring some proof

Prove| *rightful*

~~And prove~~ by ~~the book~~ that our king is dead

That all we lack is that alliance
                    this alien blood
And ~~to accept their rule instead~~ With their alien blood instead

If he died long ago

Why do you dread us so

~~The moon is out & a light~~ still throws its beam on
~~A crumbling crescent has lit the tomb~~

(   ) &c.

On F. 9*r* both stanzas I and II are crossed out, and arrows indicate that the following stanzas on F. 8*v* are to be inserted here:

Say the men of this black Tower

Though they but feed as the goat herd feeds

Their money spent & their wine gone sour

Lack nothing that a soldier needs

~~And this And that~~ That banner shall not in

                    Because not of our kin

~~The~~ This messenger that comes to buy

Swears that our own king is dead

That all we lack is their alliance

Their better law all that we need

If he died long ago

Why do they dread us so

The moon still moves its beam in the tomb

On F. 10r we hear the last of Old Tom:

climb &
~~*Old Tom the cook delights to clamber*~~
snare   in the chill of
~~*And snare small birds between night & morn*~~

~~*When all hale men better*~~
lie down in
~~*When better men are in their slumbers*~~

~~*Then an old man that goes out to*~~

~~*Old clown Tom the cock cook is proud if he clambers*~~

The tower's old cook rambles and clambers

After small birds in the chill of the morn

When all hale men are deep in their slumber

He swears that he hears our king's great horn

But he is a lying hound

We stand ~~at~~ *on the wall oath bound*

is
The moon has gone and dark the tomb

~~*The*~~ *But now comes up from the shore*

They shake when the winds roar

Old bones upon the mountain shake

With reference to the subjective and religious level of interpretation, one should notice in this draft the bread and wine in stanza I, and an oblique mention of what can only be the Bible in the line: 'And prove by the book that our rightful king is dead'. Old Tom's connexion with *King Lear* would seem to be strengthened by the reference to 'Old clown Tom'.

This poem approaches its final shape in a second manuscript draft covering three pages. F. 11r gives all but stanza III and the last refrain: the title makes its first appearance:

The Black Tower

Say that the men of this black Tower

Though they but feed as the goat herd feeds

Their money spent, their wine gone sour

Lack nothing that a soldier needs

That all are oath bound men

~~*Those that*~~

Those| ~~*That banner-s*~~ *come not in.   That banner|*

There in the tomb stand the dead upright

But wind comes up from the shore

They shake when the winds roar

Old bones upon the mountain shake

Those

~~*Their*~~ *banners come to bribe or threaten*

Or whisper that a man's a fool

Who when his own right king's forgotten

Cares what king sets up his rule

If he died long ago

Why do you dread us so

There in the tomb drops the faint moonlight

But wind comes up from the shore

They shake when the winds roar

Old bones upon the mountain shake

Stanza III is on F. 5*v*:

The tower's old cook must climb & clamber

And catch small birds in the dew of the morn

When we hale men lie stretched in slumber

~~*He*~~ *Swears that he hears the king's loud horn*

But he is a lying hound

On guard stand we oath bound

                                   stand
                                   stand the dead
And there in the tomb ~~*we stand*~~ *there upright*

And there in the tomb the moon's light

but there in the tomb it will be all dark

In this draft of the final refrain Yeats cannot escape from his own
predicament. See the emendation of what was clearly to have been
'we stand', to 'stand the dead there upright'. The dying poet is not
only thinking of his heroic 'fathers', but of himself, as he writes:
'but there in the tomb it will all be dark'. F. 12*r* shows the crystal-
lization of the final stanza and refrain:

                               that   clamber
The tower's old cook must climb & ~~ramble~~
         Catching
~~And catch~~ small birds in the dew of the morn

When we hale men lie stretched in slumber
         ~~He swears~~ Swears
~~Swore~~ that he heard the king's great horn

But he's a lying hound

Stand we on guard oath bound

There in the tomb the black grows blacker

But wind comes up from the shore

They shake when the winds roar

Old bones upon the mountain shake.

Except for punctuation and a few minor one-word alterations[1] 'The Black Tower' is now complete. The poet has so distanced himself that he appears to be narrator rather than participator. Indeed, he sounds in the opening stanza almost as if he were himself outside the black tower. The references in lines 23 and 26 to 'we hale men' and 'Stand we on guard' alone correct this impression. All superfluous and over-specific details have been winnowed away. But for the manuscript drafts we would not have heard of an 'alliance', a 'bargain', 'outlaws', the 'black pig', or even of the 'old clown Tom' who 'is crazy because of his age'. So skilful is Yeats's verbal masonry that though the reader may admire the height and proportions of 'The Black Tower', he can never hope to break into it and ransack its meaning. The stones are fitted too closely for any foothold to remain, but the manuscript drafts allow us, as it were, to look in at the lowest loophole. Our view, because it is confined, is the more fascinating: we return to the tower over and over again in the hope that we may see further. If we were to succeed, perhaps we should not come again. Everest certainly lost something of its mystery and fascination for being climbed. It is enough that we perceive that the Tower can be Yeats himself, Ireland, and a world threatened by the Third Reich. These several interpretations are complementary rather than mutually exclusive; and what of the message—in so far as such a poem has a message?

Though 'in the tomb the dark grows blacker', and the shaking of the bones can only be an evil omen, the cook, who is the one man in the tower not 'stretched in slumber', 'Swears that he hears the great king's horn'. If we were not to believe him he would not be there. Unlike us, he stands at the top of the tower, to catch the birds of heaven 'in the dew of the morn'. Can this be other than a symbol of natural regeneration? After the midnight terrors of 1939, day would break on Yeats, on Ireland, and on the world.

---

[1] On the single sheet of typescript Yeats makes the following changes:

Line 1. . . . the old black tower
     8. But winds come up . . .
    24. Swears that he hears . . .
    27. . . . the dark grows blacker

XII

CONCLUSIONS

ONE cannot assemble fractions without looking for a common denominator. I intend now to see what, if any, is the common factor shared by the poetic fractions assembled in the preceding chapters. Any answer to this question must have two headings: common factors in technique and common factors in substance. Clearly there are many places where technique and substance overlap to the extent of being inextricable, and, in a poet as skilful as Yeats, technique is always subservient to substance. Up to a point, however, they can profitably be separated for the purposes of discussion. In the course of the previous chapters I have examined the technique and substance of particular poems, often in some detail, and, if I am not now to repeat myself, must confine my remarks to generalities.

To begin with the question of technique, which I have already touched upon in my introduction, Yeats's manuscripts indicate a strong structural sense. We can never know how many preliminary drafts he may have written and thrown away: but in such poems as 'Byzantium', 'Coole Park, 1929', and 'After Long Silence', where because the sequence of the manuscript pages is more or less fixed, we appear to have the complete workings, Yeats seems to have the shape of the poem in his head before he starts. Of course he modifies it, expands one part, prunes another, in the process of composition, but never does he lose sight of his mental blue-print altogether.

This structural sense shows in his stanza-building no less than in his planning of the complete poem, for he had read enough of the sixteenth- and seventeenth-century poets to understand the importance of rhetoric. Like them he makes his poetry vertebrate with such 'figures' as the suspension at the beginning of 'After Long Silence' and at the end of 'The Gift of Harun Al-Rashid'. The three central stanzas of 'Byzantium', each of which opens with an attempted definition, are linked by the same striking syntactic pattern:

> Before me floats an image, man or shade,
> Shade more than man, more image than a shade;

> Miracle, bird or golden handiwork,
> More miracle than bird or handiwork,

> At midnight on the Emperor's pavement flit
> Flames that no faggot feeds, nor steel has lit,
> Nor storm disturbs, flames begotten of flame,

Again, he makes masterly use of repetition in building up a climax, as in 'The Second Coming':

> Surely some revelation is at hand;
> Surely the Second Coming is at hand.
> The Second Coming!

and in 'A Prayer for my Daughter':

> And for an hour I have walked and prayed
> Because of the great gloom that is in my mind.

> I have walked and prayed for this young child an hour
> And heard the sea-wind scream upon the tower,
> And under the arches of the bridge, and scream
> In the elms above the flooded stream;

If Yeats learnt his rhetoric from such poets as Spenser and Donne, he learnt from them also that rhetoric should not be obtrusive: like a good foundation it should support the house but lie beneath the ground.

Despite anything he says to the contrary in his early letters, it seems from his manuscripts as if Yeats had, at least in later life, the benefit of a great natural gift (not as common to poets as their admirers sometimes suggest)—a facility in selecting rhymes. He seems as a rule to have determined his rhyme-scheme before beginning his stanza. Sometimes, as on page 2 of 'Byzantium' and page 4 of 'Coole Park, 1929', he plots it in terms of A, B, C, D, &c. Having decided on his rhymes, however, he is quite prepared to drop them all if the stanza's substance fails to satisfy his critical standards. There are many instances of this in the preceding pages. A good example is stanza I of 'Coole Park, 1929' where, in the course of composition, every rhyme except that of the final couplet was either completely altered or changed about.

In later years Yeats came increasingly to experiment with half-rhymes, which, because they fall less heavily on the ear than full-rhymes, contribute largely to the free colloquial movement of his verse. Whereas in 'The Sorrow of Love' there are no half-rhymes, in 'Coole Park, 1929', a poem of 32 lines and, theoretically, 12 recurring rhymes, there are 11 instances of half-rhyme.

An interesting feature of the manuscripts is the word or phrase, which obviously pleases him, and which is often of central importance to the poem, that he is determined to work into its fabric somewhere. In 'Byzantium' there is 'intricacy' and 'complexity'; in 'Parting', 'declivitous/ies'. Frequently these are polysyllables, for which Yeats had a truly Irish liking: and many of his most striking effects are achieved by a resonant polysyllable following a succession of monosyllables, as for instance: 'And all the sensuality of the shade'; 'A house Where all's accustomed, ceremonious;' and 'Should the conflagration climb'. Not surprisingly this device is especially common in the last line of a stanza or a poem: 'Into the artifice of eternity'; 'That dolphin-torn, that gong-tormented sea'; 'Under the receding wave'; and 'We loved each other and were ignorant'. Like an experienced composer, Yeats knew the value of a strong closing chord to linger on in a listener's ear.

As effective as his juxtaposition of long words with short, is his use of the short line that sets off the long. 'Byzantium' is a classic example; and there is the daring finale to 'The Gift of Harun Al-Rashid':

> Of all Arabia's lovers I alone—
> Nor dazzled by the embroidery, nor lost
> In the confusion of its night-dark folds,
> Can hear the armed man speak.

Variation, of course, is an essential ingredient of good poetry: variation of pace; variation of rhythm; variation of rhyme. Yeats shows his awareness of this in his revisions, as when, in 'In Memory of Eva Gore-Booth and Con Markiewicz', he changes:

> The younger's dream makes all things seem
> The abstraction of a dream
> Her body grows skeleton-gaunt
> The symbol of her politics

to:

> I know not what the younger dreams—
> Some vague Utopia—and she seems,
> When withered old and skeleton-gaunt,
> An image of such politics.

or, in 'An Acre of Grass', when he alters:

> Now life's end draws near
> Neither loose reverie
> Nor those thoughts that hear
> Dry bone grind dry bone
> Can make the truth known.

to:

> Here at life's end
> Neither loose imagination
> Nor the mill of the mind
> Consuming its rag and bone
> Can make the truth known.

It is a significant fact that, far from working from the informal to the formal as one might imagine, Yeats tended to free his rhythms as he advanced through successive drafts of a poem. In this, as in all aspects of technique, he exemplifies the truth of the old adage: *ars est celare artem*.

To turn now to the question of substance, A. N. Jeffares has already detected one common factor:

In the majority of Yeats's poems the initial impulse was a personal emotion, often written down in the first person. As he revised the poem Yeats often removed the direct personal statement and contrived to generalize the experience slightly.[1]

Fundamentally, of course, he was a romantic poet. 'My life is in my poems', he says in his *Autobiographies*, and this is immediately obvious to even their most casual reader. From an examination of the manuscripts, however, it appears that, although many poems spring from a subjective seed, they open out into an objective flower. Mrs. Yeats says that he was aware of the danger of distorting a poem's perspective by obtruding too much the image of himself. Not that he would try to remove that image altogether. The characteristic 'I' is present at some point in the growth of all

---

[1] J. Hall and M. Steinmann, eds., *The Permanence of Yeats*, 1950, p. 304.

but one of the eighteen poems I have considered. The one exception is 'The Sorrow of Love'; but even there the intimate pronoun 'you' (which implies an 'I' figure) is dropped in favour of the more detached 'A girl arose . . .'.

Of the remaining seventeen, in four only does the first person singular pronoun not find its way into the final text. In 'Memory', 'I could not change for the grass . . .' is altered to 'Because the mountain grass', and there remains no explicit reference to the poet himself. An interesting feature of 'After Long Silence', 'The Nineteenth Century and After', and 'The Black Tower', is that the 'I' of their drafts has become 'we' in the final texts:

'After Long Silence':
  'We loved each other and were ignorant.'
'The Nineteenth Century . . .':
  'There's keen delight in what we have'.
'The Black Tower':
  'When we hale men lie stretched in slumber'.

By introducing one or more people to share the stage with him, Yeats gives these poems more of the weight and authority of universality. The reader, consciously or unconsciously, may even identify himself with the 'we' pronoun.

In two other poems containing a first person singular an 'I' is altered to 'we':

'In Memory of Eva Gore-Booth and Con Markiewicz':
  'I the great gazebo built,' became: 'We the great gazebo built,'
'Consolation':
  'I know the wisdom that there is' became: 'We fathomed all the wisdom', and finally: 'O but there is wisdom'.

A subjective element was often present in the early drafts of a poem's first stanza, and subsequently pruned or held back for a later stanza.

'Sailing to Byzantium':
  The original first stanza was abandoned for a more objective one.
'Byzantium':
  'I tread the emperor's town' was cut out.

'The Results of Thought':
   Yeats reversed the order of the opening stanzas so that the more
objective one should come first.

'An Acre of Grass':
   'My' was dropped from 'My picture & books remain'.

'A Bronze Head':
   In the finished version the poet does not introduce himself until
the third stanza.

'The Black Tower':
   The first draft began: 'I speak for the gyres of the black tower',
which later became: 'Say that the men of the old black tower . . .'.

The most dramatic reduction of the personal element is in the
development of 'A Prayer for my Daughter', where the poet re-
places three stanzas about his memories of Coole with one stanza
about his daughter—the true subject of the poem.

If 'in the majority of Yeats's poems the initial impulse was a
personal emotion', this was commonly generated by a relationship
with someone else. I can think of no other English poet who has
written so much, and so successfully, about so many individual
people. A love-poet will, of course, write about his beloved, but
in Yeats, more than most poets, kinship and friendship had the
power of spurring him to song.

> Think where man's glory most begins and ends,
> And say my glory was I had such friends.

Maud Gonne, Lady Gregory, Anne Gregory, Major Robert Gregory, Hugh Lane, Mabel Beardsley, Dorothy Wellesley: for and
concerning these he wrote much of his finest poetry. He romanti-
cized them, of course, cast their images in verbal bronze, giving
them the larger-than-life-size stature of mythological figures. This
he did because his vision was essentially dramatic. His early
interest in the heroic mythology of Ireland, and his long association
with the Abbey Theatre had given him an eye for the dramatic
figure, gesture, and situation. Hence his love for the proud past,
his despair at the ignoble and materialist present, and—sometimes—his hope for a future that would rediscover the traditional

values. Almost everything he wrote, poetry, essay, and play, was dedicated to the task of restoring these ancient heroic values.

> We were the last romantics—chose for theme
> Traditional sanctity and loveliness;
> Whatever's written in what poet's name
> The book of the people; whatever most can bless
> The mind of man or elevate a rhyme;
> But all is changed, that high horse riderless,
> Though mounted in that saddle Homer rode
> Where the swan drifts upon a darkening flood.

He was intensely aware of people. Not, however, as Shakespeare and Chaucer were aware of them; seeing them for what they were, and delighting in what they saw, irrespective of whether it was ugly or beautiful, ludicrous or sublime. Yeats's vision, as I have already said, was romantic rather than realist. He saw what he wanted to see in people: the wise man lurking in the fool, the hero in 'the drunken vainglorious lout'. In this, as in all things, he was creative.

It is interesting to see how many of the poems are either centred on an 'I' figure and one or more others, or appear (from their early drafts) to have been prompted by individual people: the latter are often types:

'The Second Coming':
    'The germans are to Russia come'. Pitt, Burke, mob, murderer, judge, tyrant, anarch, all pass through the early manuscript drafts.
'A Prayer for my Daughter':
    Anne Yeats and Maud Gonne.
'The Sorrow of Love':
    Maud Gonne.
'The Gift of Harun Al-Rashid':
    The poet and his wife disguised as Kusta Ben Luka and his bride.
'Sailing to Byzantium':
    Those that Yeats loved in his first youth: the Danish Merchant. The poet's journey is between 'The young in one another's arms' and 'lords and ladies of Byzantium'.
'Byzantium':
    Soldier, robber, victim, harlot.

'Chosen' and 'Parting':
 'I' and 'he', (the lady and her lover).

'In Memory of Eva Gore-Booth and Con Markiewicz':
 The two ladies in the title.

'Coole Park, 1929':
 Lady Gregory, Douglas Hyde, John Synge, Shawe-Taylor, and Hugh Lane.

'Memory':
 Olivia Shakespeare (?)

'Consolation':
 Olivia Shakespeare (?)

'After Long Silence':
 Olivia Shakespeare (?)

'The Nineteenth Century and After':
 'the great men'.

'The Results of Thought':

> Friends ignorant & blind
> Wrecked lives, a woman there
> Of all wrecks there the worst

'An Acre of Grass':
 Timon, Lear, William Blake, Michael Angelo.

Doggerel ballad:
 Lady, lover, and Billy Boy.

'A Bronze Head':
 Maud Gonne, McTaggart.

'The Black Tower':
 Old Tom/cook, king, soldiers, messenger, goatherd.

That thirteen out of eighteen poems (something over two-thirds) should have originated from women, is a significant—and not, I think, an unrepresentative—proportion. It is also interesting to see how many of the poems are retrospective. The head turned over the shoulder is, perhaps, the most common of poetic attitudes: and one of which Yeats, with his reverence for the past, was particularly fond. It is true that only one of the poems with which I am concerned was written before 1919, and one might reasonably expect a man of over fifty to be somewhat retrospective. Even before the turn of the century, however, he was writing such poems as 'The Falling of the Leaves', 'Down by the Salley Gardens', and 'The Meditation of the Old Fisherman'.

In striking contrast to Yeats's retrospective attitude is the prophetic and forward-looking attitude of 'The Second Coming', 'Sailing to Byzantium', 'Byzantium', and 'The Black Tower'. Here he is at his best, because like one of the old heroes he admired so much, he can face the terror of the unknown with courage and resolution. It is no coincidence that soldiers feature in 'The Second Coming', 'Byzantium', lines cancelled from 'Two Voices', and 'The Black Tower'.

Although Yeats was not a Christian, nor for any appreciable period a member of any religious sect—I believe consciously or subconsciously he felt dependence on a deity to be weakness—he had a lively religious curiosity. This is not surprising in someone so fascinated by traditional learning and problems of the past and future. As a young man he seems to have been interested in the drama and ritual of the Christian church. He used its symbols in 'The Secret Rose', 'The Travail of Passion', and 'The Lover speaks to the Hearers of his Songs in Coming Days'; and later in two plays, *Calvary* (1920) and *The Resurrection* (1931). Throughout his life, religion in general, and Christianity in particular, had a magnetic attraction for him, both aesthetically and morally: almost in spite of himself, he turned to them over and over again. Anxious though he was to avoid the stigma of orthodoxy, it is interesting to see revealed the religious thread running through so many of his poems. 'The Second Coming' and 'A Prayer for my Daughter' are obvious examples. There are deity-symbols at the centre of 'The Gift of Harun Al-Rashid', 'Sailing to Byzantium', and 'Byzantium': and the sages, which I have suggested carry religious associations for Yeats, appear in 'Sailing to Byzantium', 'In Memory of Eva Gore-Booth and Con Markiewicz', 'Coole Park, 1929', and 'Consolation'. Finally, there is 'The Black Tower', which on one level I believe to be a religious poem.

An important and consistent feature of Yeats's revision is his tendency to cut the material with which he begins: seldom to add to it. He works inwards towards a centre, rather than outwards and away from it. As I have suggested earlier in this chapter, he tended to prune particular detail, thus making the finished design more objective. This appears in several poems:

'The Second Coming':
  Germans, Russia, Burke, Pitt, gown, mob, murderer, judge, dock, tyrant, anarch, make way for the powerful and prophetic lines:

> Mere anarchy is loosed upon the world,
> The blood-dimmed tide is loosed, and everywhere
> The ceremony of innocence is drowned;

  In line 18, the image of the dark 'rent as it were cloth' and 'cut as with a knife' is replaced by the more simple 'The darkness drops again;'

'A Prayer for my Daughter':
  From stanza I are dropped the details of the cradle's age and 'broidered coverlid'. Finally, stanzas X, XI, and XII, with their detailed vision of Coole, are exchanged for a single stanza in which are tied together the true themes of the poem.

'Sailing to Byzantium':
  The original opening stanza, with its obvious Irish details, was abandoned in its entirety. Abandoned also are the 'dark skinned mariners', 'the Danish merchant', and the physical details of Byzantium; statue, stair, mirroring waters, sail, oar, jetty, and the dolphins that were to reappear in 'Byzantium'.

'Chosen' and 'Parting':
  The forty lines of parts II and III are cut and rejected.

'In Memory of Eva Gore-Booth and Con Markiewicz':
  From part II are dropped the details of the bellows, and the cradles that Nature still has left to fill.

'Coole Park, 1929':
  The original stanza IV, with its religious overtones, is abandoned.

'After Long Silence':
  All mention of the white hair of the poet and his beloved has vanished from the final text.

'The Black Tower':
  The Black Pig's dike/banner, Old Tom, and the messenger are abandoned.

Although outside the scope of the present study, it is worth noting
that complete stanzas have been dropped from 'Coole Park and
Ballylee, 1931'[1] and 'The Circus Animals' Desertion'.[2]

On the evidence then of eighteen poems, it would seem that
Yeats generally began to write on a subjective note, but often
worked himself into the background as he proceeded. Personal
relationships—especially with women—were a common theme.
Both he and the figures depicted in these relationships were painted
with the primary colours of Romance. He was passionately concerned with the traditional values of the past and the dark portents
of the future; and was fascinated by the problems and possibilities
of religion. His manuscripts show constant evidence of the pruning
knife, judiciously used on any dead wood and inessential detail:
they show that of all the tools in the poet's workshop the most
important is a razor-sharp self-critical faculty.

[1] *Variorum*, p. 491.   [2] p. 221.

SELECT BIBLIOGRAPHY

WORKS BY W. B. YEATS

Unpublished Material

1. Manuscripts for plays, poems, and prose in the possession of Mrs. W. B. Yeats.
2. A number of manuscript books, four of which I have referred to and called:
   - A. A small, squat book, measuring 19 × 11 cm., in a worn and faded embroidered cover, inscribed on the fly-leaf: 'W. B. Yeats/August 29th/1893.' This contains drafts of many poems later included in *The Wind Among the Reeds.*
   - B. A book measuring 30 × 22 cm., with a patterned cover cracked at the spine. It was begun at Rapallo in 1928, and contains drafts of poems later included in *The Winding Stair and Other Poems.*
   - C. A white, vellum-bound book, measuring 34·5 × 21 cm., begun on 23 November 1930. This contains, amongst a mass of other material, drafts of poems later included in *The Winding Stair and Other Poems* and *A Full Moon in March.*
   - D. A brown leather book, measuring 25 × 16·5 cm., with three stamped hinges. This is inscribed on the fly-leaf: 'Rapallo. June 1934', and contains drafts of poems later included in *A Full Moon in March.*
3. Two letters from Yeats to Mr. T. Mark, of Macmillan & Co., Ltd.

Published Works

The Works of William Blake, Bernard Quaritch, 1893.
Poems of Spenser, T. C. & E. C. Jack, 1906.
Collected Works in Verse and Prose, Shakespeare Head Press, 1908.
Plays and Controversies, Macmillan, 1923.
Essays, Macmillan, 1924.
A Vision, T. Werner Laurie, 1925.
A Packet for Ezra Pound, Cuala Press, 1929.
Wheels and Butterflies, Macmillan, 1934.
The Oxford Book of Modern Verse/1892–1935, Chosen by W. B. Yeats, Oxford, 1936.
A Vision, Macmillan, 1937.
Essays/1931–1936, Cuala Press, 1937.
On the Boiler, Cuala Press, 1939.
Collected Plays, Macmillan, 1952.
Autobiographies, Macmillan, 1955.
Variorum Edition of the Poems, Macmillan, 1957.

Published Letters

BAX, C., ed. *Florence Farr, Bernard Shaw and W. B. Yeats*, Cuala Press, 1941.
BRIDGE, U., ed. *W. B. Yeats and T. Sturge Moore/Their Correspondence/1901–1937*. Routledge & Kegan Paul, 1953.
WADE, A., ed. *The Letters of W. B. Yeats*. Macmillan, 1954.
WELLESLEY, D., ed. *Letters on Poetry from W. B. Yeats to Dorothy Wellesley*. Oxford Univ. Press, 1940.

For a bibliography of books and articles by other authors (up to 1957) see:
SAUL, G. B. *Prolegomena to the Study of Yeats's Poems*, Philadelphia Univ. Press, 1957.

INDEX

Abbreviation: 'n.' after page no. refers to a footnote

Titan, 22.
Tom, Old, *see* Old Tom.
Trade Union Movement, 167.
Transport Workers' Union, 167.
'Travail of Passion, The', 251.
Trembling of the Veil, The, 185.
Tuatha De Danaan, 92, 229.
'Twelfth Elegy', 143.
'Two Voices', 140–1, 161, 251.
'Tyger', 122.
Tynan, Katherine, 1.

Unicorn, 159–61.
Unseen Kings, 166.
'Upon a Dying Lady', 205.

'Vacillation', 65.
'Valley of the Black Pig, The', 228.
Variorum Edition of the Poems of W. B. Yeats, 13, 15, 18 n., 63 n., 69 n., 81–82, 100 n., 151 n., 174, 228 n.–229 n., 253 n.
Vaughan, Henry, 131.
Vestal, 97–98, 112.
Virgil, 44, 101 n., 119.
Vision, A, 18, 21, 50, 60, 62, 65, 83, 85, 101, 109, 125, 146, 152.
Visions and Beliefs in the West of Ireland, 123.
Vogelweide, Walther von der, 142.
Volpone, 143.

Wade, A., ed., *The Letters of W. B. Yeats*, 1 n., 5 n.–7 n., 9 n., 12 n., 14 n., 208 n., 211 n.
'Wanderings of Oisin, The', 1, 8, 14, 49.
Wanderings of Oisin and Other Poems, The, 4.
Weeks, D., 'Image and Idea in Yeats's "The Second Coming" ', 23.
Wellesley, Dorothy, 5–6, 248.
'Wheel, The', 7.

'Wheel and the Phases of the Moon, The', *see* 'Phases of the Moon, The'.
Wheels and Butterflies, 23.
'Wild Swans at Coole, The', 44.
Wilde, Lady, 228.
Wilde, Oscar, 62.
Wilson, F. A. C., *Yeats's Iconography*, 35.
Wind Among the Reeds, The, 9, 85.
Winding Stair and Other Poems, The, 125, 151, 168, 200.
Woburn Buildings, 4, 205, 223.
'Woman Young and Old, A', 139, 168.
Women's Suffrage Movement, 166.
'Words for Music Perhaps', 236.
Wordsworth, William, 1.

Yasmin, Yasmine, 62, 65.
Yeats, Anne, 29, 44, 249.
Yeats, Lily, 14.
Yeats, Mrs. W. B., v, 4, 6–9, 12–14, 17, 60–61, 85, 89, 96–97, 200, 211, 223, 227, 229, 232, 236, 246; automatic writing, 62, 79, 83; in Sicily, 97.
Yeats, W. B., attempted destruction of rough drafts, v, 9, 17; diary, 97 n., 115, 126; friendship with Lady Gregory, 178; in Sicily, 97; learnt his Arabic, 60; method of composition, 1, 4–7, 9–14; orthography, 9, 11–12; philosophical system, 69, 83, 115; reduction of particular detail, 251–2, the subjective element, 246–50; use of polysyllables, 245, rhetoric, 243–4, rhyme, 244–5, rhythm, 8–9, 246; views on Christianity, 251, contemporary poetry, 211–12, music, 7–8, symbolism, 85. *See also* separate entries for individual poems.

Zeus, 21, 72.
Zodiac, 137, 151–2, 158, 160–1.

PRINTED IN GREAT BRITAIN
AT THE UNIVERSITY PRESS, OXFORD
BY VIVIAN RIDLER
PRINTER TO THE UNIVERSITY

DATE DUE
